Colors, Backgrounds, and Gradients

Eric A. Meyer

Beijing · Cambridge · Farnham · Köln · Sebastopol · Tokyo

Colors, Backgrounds, and Gradients

by Eric A. Meyer

Copyright © 2015 Eric A. Meyer. All rights reserved.

Printed in the United States of America.

Published by O'Reilly Media, Inc., 1005 Gravenstein Highway North, Sebastopol, CA 95472.

O'Reilly books may be purchased for educational, business, or sales promotional use. Online editions are also available for most titles (*http://safaribooksonline.com*). For more information, contact our corporate/institutional sales department: 800-998-9938 or corporate@oreilly.com.

Editors: Simon St.Laurent and Meg Foley
Production Editor: Colleen Lobner
Copyeditor: Sonia Saruba
Proofreader: Amanda Kersey

Interior Designer: David Futato
Cover Designer: Ellie Volckhausen
Illustrator: Rebecca Demarest

June 2015:   First Edition

Revision History for the First Edition
2015-05-29:   First Release
2015-06-22:   Second Release

See *http://oreilly.com/catalog/errata.csp?isbn=9781491927656* for release details.

978-1-491-92765-6

[LSI]

Table of Contents

Preface

Conventions Used in This Book

The following typographical conventions are used in this book:

Italic
> Indicates new terms, URLs, email addresses, filenames, and file extensions.

`Constant width`
> Used for program listings, as well as within paragraphs to refer to program elements such as variable or function names, databases, data types, environment variables, statements, and keywords.

`Constant width bold`
> Shows commands or other text that should be typed literally by the user.

`Constant width italic`
> Shows text that should be replaced with user-supplied values or by values determined by context.

> This element signifies a general note.

> This element indicates a warning or caution.

Using Code Examples

This book is here to help you get your job done. In general, if example code is offered with this book, you may use it in your programs and documentation. You do not need to contact us for permission unless you're reproducing a significant portion of the code. For example, writing a program that uses several chunks of code from this book does not require permission. Selling or distributing a CD-ROM of examples from O'Reilly books does require permission. Answering a question by citing this book and quoting example code does not require permission. Incorporating a significant amount of example code from this book into your product's documentation does require permission.

We appreciate, but do not require, attribution. An attribution usually includes the title, author, publisher, and ISBN. For example: "*Colors, Backgrounds, and Gradients* by Eric A. Meyer (O'Reilly). Copyright 2015 Eric A. Meyer, 978-1-491-92765-6."

If you feel your use of code examples falls outside fair use or the permission given above, feel free to contact us at *permissions@oreilly.com*.

Safari® Books Online

Safari Books Online is an on-demand digital library that delivers expert content in both book and video form from the world's leading authors in technology and business.

Technology professionals, software developers, web designers, and business and creative professionals use Safari Books Online as their primary resource for research, problem solving, learning, and certification training.

Safari Books Online offers a range of plans and pricing for enterprise, government, education, and individuals.

Members have access to thousands of books, training videos, and prepublication manuscripts in one fully searchable database from publishers like O'Reilly Media, Prentice Hall Professional, Addison-Wesley Professional, Microsoft Press, Sams, Que, Peachpit Press, Focal Press, Cisco Press, John Wiley & Sons, Syngress, Morgan Kaufmann, IBM Redbooks, Packt, Adobe Press, FT Press, Apress, Manning, New Riders, McGraw-Hill, Jones & Bartlett, Course Technology, and hundreds more. For more information about Safari Books Online, please visit us online.

How to Contact Us

Please address comments and questions concerning this book to the publisher:

O'Reilly Media, Inc.
1005 Gravenstein Highway North
Sebastopol, CA 95472
800-998-9938 (in the United States or Canada)
707-829-0515 (international or local)
707-829-0104 (fax)

We have a web page for this book, where we list errata, examples, and any additional information. You can access this page at *http://bit.ly/colors-backgrounds-gradients*.

To comment or ask technical questions about this book, send email to *bookquestions@oreilly.com*.

For more information about our books, courses, conferences, and news, see our website at *http://www.oreilly.com*.

Find us on Facebook: *http://facebook.com/oreilly*

Follow us on Twitter: *http://twitter.com/oreillymedia*

Watch us on YouTube: *http://www.youtube.com/oreillymedia*

Colors and Backgrounds

Remember the first time you changed the colors of a web page? Instead of the default black text on a white background with blue links, all of a sudden you could use any combination of colors you desired—perhaps light blue text on a black background with lime green hyperlinks. From there, it was just a short hop to colored text and, eventually, even to multiple colors for the text in a page. Once you could add background images, too, just about anything became possible, or so it seemed. Cascading Style Sheets (CSS) takes color and backgrounds even further, letting you apply many different colors and backgrounds to a single page or element, and even apply multiple backgrounds to the same element.

Colors

When you're designing a page, you need to plan it out before you start. That's generally true in any case, but with colors, it's even more so. If you're going to make all hyperlinks yellow, will that clash with the background color in any part of your document? If you use too many colors, will the user be too overwhelmed? (Hint: yes.) If you change the default hyperlink colors, will users still be able to figure out where your links are? (For example, if you make both regular text and hyperlink text the same color, it will be much harder to spot links—in fact, almost impossible if the links aren't underlined.)

There is really only one type of color in CSS, and that's a plain, solid color. If you set the color of a document to be red, then the text will be the same shade of red. If you use CSS to set the color of all hyperlinks (both visited and unvisited) to be blue, then that's most likely what they'll be. In the same way, if you use styles to set the background of the body to be green, then the entire body background will be the same shade of green.

In CSS, you can set both the foreground and background colors of any element. In order to understand how this works, it's important to understand what's in the foreground of an element and what isn't. Generally speaking, it's the text of an element, although the foreground also includes the borders around the element. Thus, there are two ways to directly affect the foreground color of an element: by using the color property, and by setting the border colors using one of a number of border properties.

Foreground Colors

The easiest way to set the foreground color of an element is with the property color.

<table>
<tr><td colspan="2" align="center">**color**</td></tr>
<tr><td>**Values:**</td><td>`<color>|inherit`</td></tr>
<tr><td>**Initial value:**</td><td>User agent-specific</td></tr>
<tr><td>**Applies to:**</td><td>All elements</td></tr>
<tr><td>**Inherited:**</td><td>Yes</td></tr>
<tr><td>**Computed value:**</td><td>As specified</td></tr>
</table>

This property accepts as a value any valid color type, such as `#FFCC00` or `rgba(100%, 80%,0%,0.5)`.

For nonreplaced elements, color sets the color of the text in the element, as illustrated in Figure 1, which is the result of the following code:

```
<p style="color: gray;">This paragraph has a gray foreground.</p>
<p>This paragraph has the default foreground.</p>
```

This paragraph has a gray foreground.

This paragraph has the default foreground.

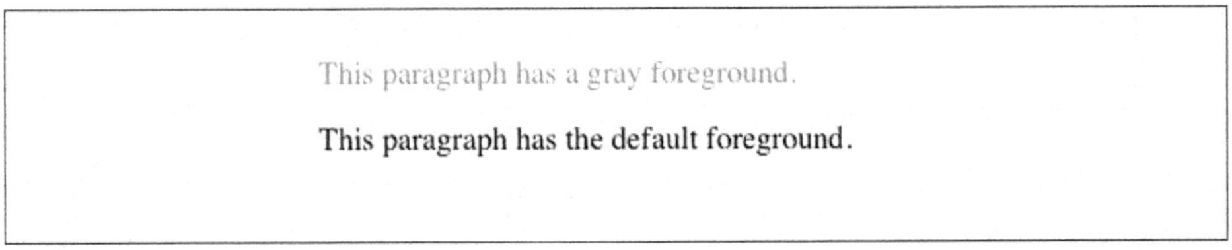

Figure 1. Declared color versus default color

In Figure 1, the default foreground color is black. That doesn't have to be the case, since the user might have set her browser (or other user agent) to use a different foreground (text) color. If the browser's default text color was set to green, the second paragraph in the preceding example would be green, not black—but the first paragraph would still be gray.

You need not restrict yourself to such simple operations, of course. There are plenty of ways to use `color`. You might have some paragraphs that contain text warning the user of a potential problem. In order to make this text stand out more than usual, you might decide to color it red. Simply apply a class of `warn` to each paragraph that contains warning text (`<p class="warn">`) and the following rule:

```
p.warn {color: red;}
```

In the same document, you might decide that any unvisited hyperlinks within a warning paragraph should be green:

```
p.warn {color: red;}
p.warn a:link {color: green;}
```

Then you change your mind, deciding that warning text should be dark red, and that unvisited links in such text should be medium purple. The preceding rules need only be changed to reflect the new values, as illustrated in Figure 2, which is the result of the following code:

```
p.warn {color: #600;}
p.warn a:link {color: #400040;}
```

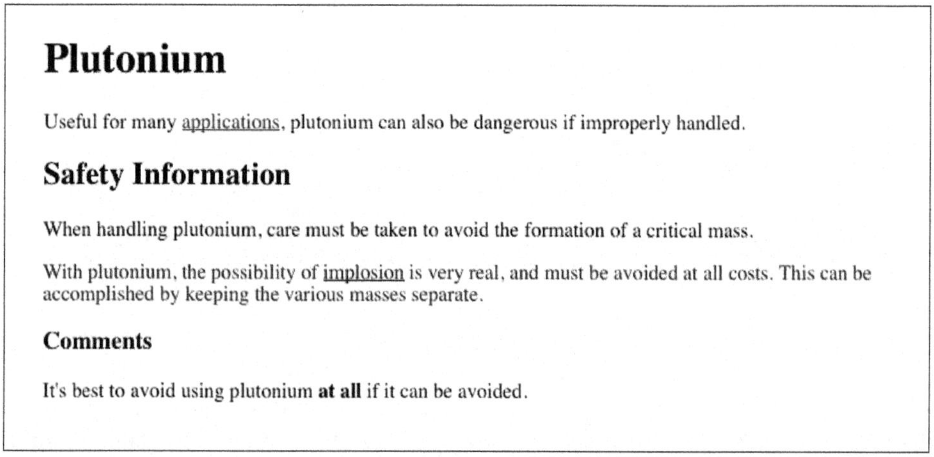

Plutonium

Useful for many applications, plutonium can also be dangerous if improperly handled.

Safety Information

When handling plutonium, care must be taken to avoid the formation of a critical mass.

With plutonium, the possibility of implosion is very real, and must be avoided at all costs. This can be accomplished by keeping the various masses separate.

Comments

It's best to avoid using plutonium **at all** if it can be avoided.

Figure 2. Changing colors

Another use for `color` is to draw attention to certain types of text. For example, bold-faced text is already fairly obvious, but you could give it a different color to make it stand out even further—let's say, maroon:

```
b, strong {color: maroon;}
```

Then you decide that you want all table cells with a class of `highlight` to contain light yellow text:

```
td.highlight {color: #FF9;}
```

Of course, if you don't set a background color for any of your text, you run the risk that a user's setup won't combine well with your own. For example, if a user has set his browser's background to be a pale yellow, like #FFC, then the previous rule would generate light yellow text on a pale yellow background. Far more likely is that it's still the default background of white, against which light yellow is still going to be hard to read. It's therefore generally a good idea to set foreground and background colors together. (We'll talk about background colors very shortly.)

Affecting Borders

The value of `color` can also affect the borders around an element. Let's assume you've declared these styles, which have the result shown in Figure 3. This is the result of the following code:

```
p.aside {color: gray; border-style: solid;}
```

Fire as Urban Renewal

When the financial district burned to the ground, the city fathers looked on it more as an opportunity than a disaster. Here was an opportunity to do things right. Here was their big chance to finally build a city that would be functional, clean, and attractive. Or at least not flooded with sewage every high tide.

Although the man who started the fire fled town, there's some speculation that he might have been lauded for giving the city an excuse to start over.

A plan was quickly conceived and approved. The fathers got together with the merchants and explained it. "Here's what we'll do," they said, "we'll raise the ground level of the financial district well above the high-tide line. We're going to cart all the dirt we need down from the hills, fill in the entire area, even build a real sewer system. Once we've done that you can rebuild your businesses on dry, solid ground. What do you think?"

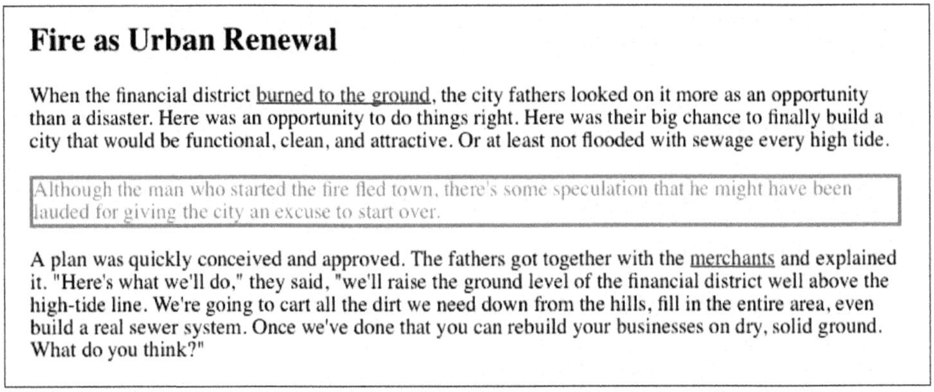

Figure 3. Border colors are taken from the content's color

The element `<p class="aside">` has gray text and a gray medium-width solid border. This is because the foreground color is applied to the borders by default. Should you desire, you can override this with the property `border-color`:

```
p.aside {color: gray; border-style: solid; border-color: black;}
```

This rule will make the text gray, while the borders will be black in color. Any value set for `border-color` will always override the value of `color`.

The borders, incidentally, allow you to affect the foreground color of images. Since images are already composed of colors, you can't really affect them using `color`, but you can change the color of any border that appears around the image. This can be done using either `color` or `border-color`. Therefore, the following rules will have the same visual effect on images of class `type1` *and* `type2`, as shown in Figure 4, which is the result of the following code:

```
img.type1 {color: gray; border-style: solid;}
img.type2 {border-color: gray; border-style: solid;}
```

Figure 4. Setting the border color for images

Affecting Form Elements

Setting a value for `color` should (in theory, anyway) apply to form elements. Declaring `select` elements to have dark gray text should be as simple as this:

```
select {color: rgb(33%,33%,33%);}
```

This might also set the color of the borders around the edge of the `select` element, or it might not. It all depends on the user agent and its default styles.

You can also set the foreground color of input elements—although, as you can see in Figure 5, doing so would apply that color to all inputs, from text to radio button to checkbox inputs:

```
select {color: rgb(33%,33%,33%);}
input {color: red;}
```

Figure 5. Changing form element foregrounds

Note in Figure 5 that the text color next to the checkboxes is still black. This is because the rules shown assign styles only to elements like `input` and `select`, not normal paragraph (or other) text.

Also note that the checkmark in the checkbox is black. This is due to the way form elements are handled in some web browsers, which typically use the form widgets built into the base operating system. Thus, when you see a checkbox and checkmark, they really aren't content in the HTML document—they're content that has been inserted into the document, much as an image would be. In fact, form inputs are, like images, replaced elements. In theory, CSS does not style the contents of replaced elements.

In practice, the line is a lot blurrier than that, as Figure 5 demonstrates. Some form inputs have the color of their text and even portions of their UI changed, while others do not. And since the rules aren't explicitly defined, behavior is inconsistent across browsers. Some may present a red checkmark, while others will not. In short, form elements are deeply tricky to style and should be approached with extreme caution.

Inheriting Color

As the definition of color indicates, the property is inherited. This makes sense, since if you declare p {color: gray;}, you probably expect that any text within that paragraph will also be gray, even if it's emphasized or boldfaced or whatever. Of course, if you *want* such elements to be different colors, that's easy enough, as illustrated in Figure 6, which is the result of the following code:

```
em {color: red;}
p {color: gray;}
```

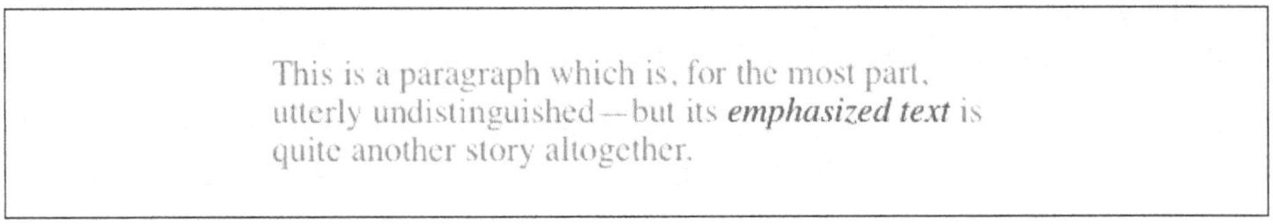

> This is a paragraph which is, for the most part, utterly undistinguished — but its *emphasized text* is quite another story altogether.

Figure 6. Different colors for different elements

Since color is inherited, it's theoretically possible to set all of the ordinary text in a document to a color, such as red, by declaring body {color: red;}. This should make all text that is not otherwise styled (such as anchors, which have their own color styles) red.

Backgrounds

By default, the background area of an element consists of all of the space behind the foreground out to the outer edge of the borders; thus, the content box and the padding are all part of an element's background, and the borders are drawn on top of the background. (You can change that to a degree with CSS, as we'll see shortly.)

CSS lets you apply a solid color or create moderately sophisticated effects using background images, and its capabilities in this area far outstrip those of HTML. And that's without even getting into the new ability to apply multiple background images to a single element, including linear and radial gradients.

Background Colors

It's possible to declare a color for the background of an element, in a fashion very similar to setting the foreground color. For this, you use the property background-color, which accepts (unsurprisingly) any valid color or a keyword that makes the background transparent.

<table>
<tr><td colspan="2" align="center">background-color</td></tr>
<tr><td>Values:</td><td><code><color>|transparent|inherit</code></td></tr>
<tr><td>Initial value:</td><td><code>transparent</code></td></tr>
<tr><td>Applies to:</td><td>All elements</td></tr>
<tr><td>Inherited:</td><td>No</td></tr>
<tr><td>Computed value:</td><td>As specified</td></tr>
</table>

If you want the color to extend out a little bit from the text in the element, simply add some padding to the mix, as illustrated in Figure 7, which is the result of the following code:

```
p.padded {background-color: #AEA; padding: 1em;}
```

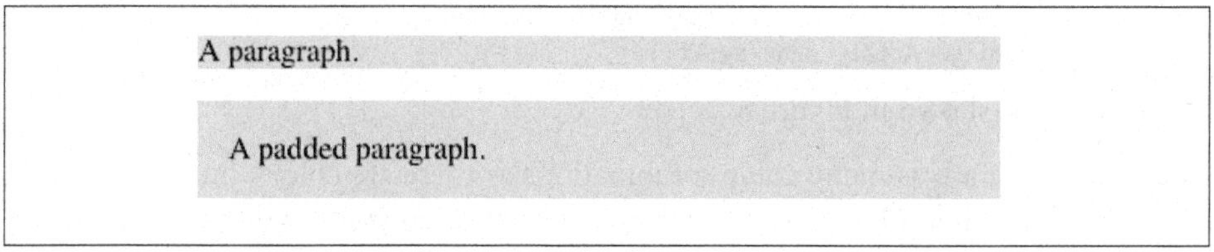

Figure 7. Backgrounds and padding

You can set a background color for just about any element, from body all the way down to inline elements such as em and a. The background-color is not inherited. Its default value is transparent, which makes sense: if an element doesn't have a defined color, then its background should be transparent so that the background of its ancestor elements will be visible.

One way to picture what that means is to imagine a clear (i.e., transparent) plastic sign mounted to a textured wall. The wall is still visible through the sign, but this is not the background of the sign; it's the background of the wall (in CSS terms, anyway). Similarly, if you set the page canvas to have a background, it can be seen through all of the elements in the document that don't have their own backgrounds. They don't inherit the background; it is visible *through* them. This may seem like an irrelevant distinction, but as you'll see when we discuss background images, it's actually a critical difference.

Most of the time, you'll have no reason to use the keyword `transparent`, since that's the default value. On occasion, though, it can be useful. Imagine that a user has set his browser to make all links have a white background. When you design your page, you set anchors to have a white foreground, and you don't want a background on those anchors. In order to make sure your design choice prevails, you would declare:

```
a {color: white; background-color: transparent;}
```

If you left out the background color, your white foreground would combine with the user's white background to yield totally unreadable links. This is an unlikely example, but it's still possible.

The potential combination of author and reader styles is the reason why a CSS validator will generate warnings such as, "You have no `background-color` with your `color`." It's trying to remind you that author-user color interaction can occur, and your rule has not taken this possibility into account. Warnings do not mean your styles are invalid: only errors prevent validation.

Special effects

Simply by combining `color` and `background-color`, you can create some interesting effects:

```
h1 {color: white; background-color: rgb(20%,20%,20%);
    font-family: Arial, sans-serif;}
```

This example is shown in Figure 8.

Of course, there are as many color combinations as there are colors, but I can't show all of them here. Still, I'll try to give you some idea of what you can do.

This stylesheet is a little more complicated, as illustrated by Figure 9, which is the result of the following code:

```
body {color: black; background-color: white;}
h1, h2 {color: yellow; background-color: rgb(0,51,0);}
p {color: #555;}
a:link {color: black; background-color: silver;}
a:visited {color: gray; background-color: white;}
```

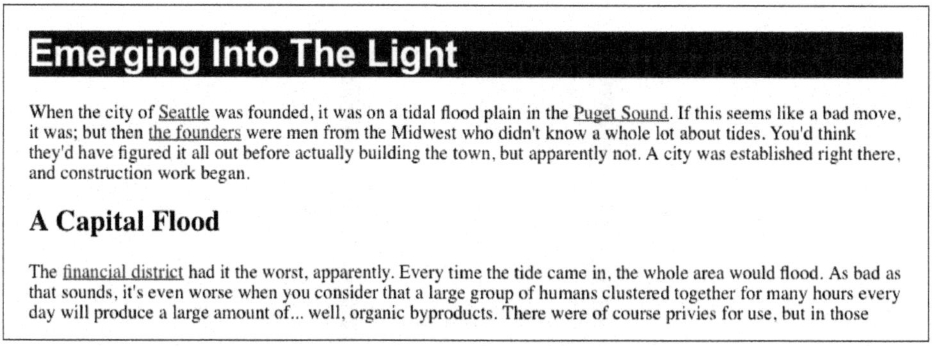

Emerging Into The Light

When the city of Seattle was founded, it was on a tidal flood plain in the Puget Sound. If this seems like a bad move, it was; but then the founders were men from the Midwest who didn't know a whole lot about tides. You'd think they'd have figured it all out before actually building the town, but apparently not. A city was established right there, and construction work began.

A Capital Flood

The financial district had it the worst, apparently. Every time the tide came in, the whole area would flood. As bad as that sounds, it's even worse when you consider that a large group of humans clustered together for many hours every day will produce a large amount of... well, organic byproducts. There were of course privies for use, but in those

Figure 8. A reverse-text effect for H1 elements

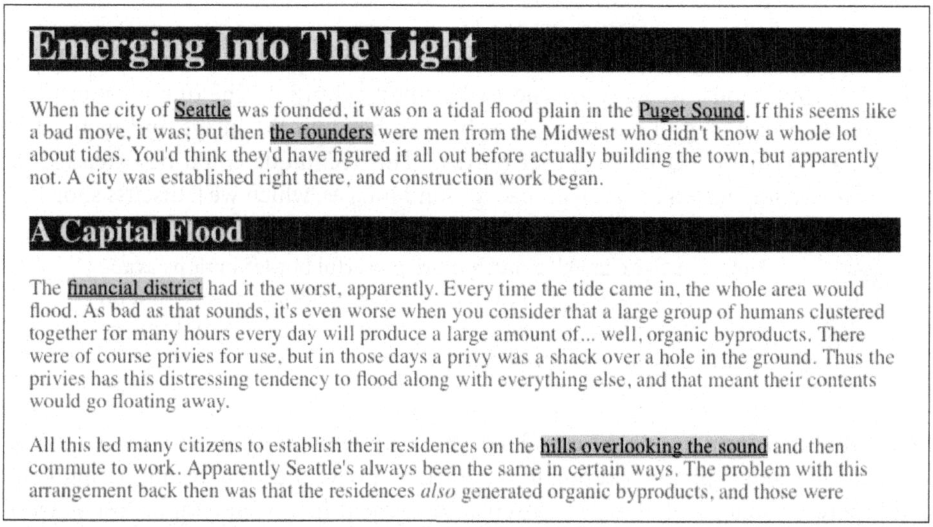

Emerging Into The Light

When the city of Seattle was founded, it was on a tidal flood plain in the Puget Sound. If this seems like a bad move, it was; but then the founders were men from the Midwest who didn't know a whole lot about tides. You'd think they'd have figured it all out before actually building the town, but apparently not. A city was established right there, and construction work began.

A Capital Flood

The financial district had it the worst, apparently. Every time the tide came in, the whole area would flood. As bad as that sounds, it's even worse when you consider that a large group of humans clustered together for many hours every day will produce a large amount of... well, organic byproducts. There were of course privies for use, but in those days a privy was a shack over a hole in the ground. Thus the privies has this distressing tendency to flood along with everything else, and that meant their contents would go floating away.

All this led many citizens to establish their residences on the hills overlooking the sound and then commute to work. Apparently Seattle's always been the same in certain ways. The problem with this arrangement back then was that the residences *also* generated organic byproducts, and those were

Figure 9. The results of a more complicated stylesheet

And then there's the fascinating question of what happens when you apply a background to a replaced element, such as an image. I'm not even talking about images with transparent portions, like a GIF87a or a PNG. Suppose you want to create a two-tone border around a JPEG. You can pull that off by adding a background color and a little bit of padding to your image, as illustrated in Figure 10, which is the result of the following code:

```
img.twotone {background-color: red; padding: 5px; border: 5px solid gold;}
```

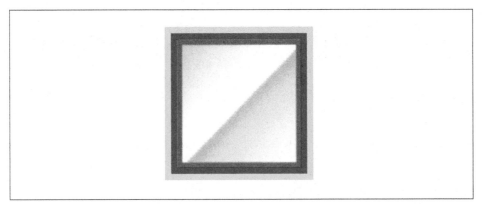

Figure 10. Using background and border to two-tone an image

Technically, the background goes to the outer border edge, but since the border is solid and continuous, we can't see the background behind it. The one pixel of padding allows a thin ring of background to be seen between the image and its border, creating the visual effect of an "inner border." This technique could be extended to create more complicated effects with background images, which we'll discuss shortly.

 Note that there are also much more powerful border options available in CSS, so background-and-padding tricks may or may not be useful, depending on what you want to do and the state of browser support for the advanced border options.

Remember that form inputs, nearly all of which are replaced elements, are treated as special, and often applying padding to them will not have the same results as applying padding to an image, let alone a nonreplaced element like a paragraph. Just as with most styling of form inputs, adding a background color should be rigorously tested and avoided if possible.

Clipping the Background

In the previous section, we saw how backgrounds fill out the entire background area of an element. Historically, that extended all the way to the outer edge of the border so that any border with transparent parts (like dashed or dotted borders) would have the background color fill into those transparent parts. Well, there's a new CSS property called `background-clip` that lets you affect how far out an element's background will go.

---

background-clip

Values:	[*<box>* [, *<box>*]*]	inherit
Initial value:	*<box>* = border-box	padding-box	content-box
Applies to:	All elements
Inherited:	No
Computed value:	As declared

The default value is the historical value: the *background painting area* (which is what `background-clip` defines) extends out to the outer edge of the border. The background will *always* be drawn behind the visible parts of the border, if any.

If you choose the value `padding-box`, then the background will only extend to the outer edge of the padding area (which is also the inner edge of the border). Thus, it won't be drawn behind the border. The value `content-box`, on the other hand, restricts the background to just the content area of the element.

The effects of these three values is illustrated in Figure 11, which is the result of the following code:

```
div[id] {color: navy; background: silver;
         padding: 1em; border: 5px dashed;}
#ex01 {background-clip: border-box;}   /* default value */
#ex02 {background-clip: padding-box;}
#ex03 {background-clip: content-box;}
```

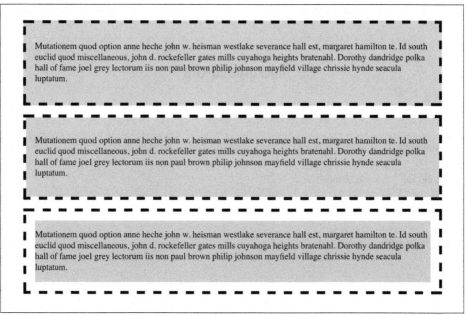

Figure 11. The three types of background clipping

That seems pretty simple, but there are some caveats. The first is that `background-clip` has no effect on the root element (in HTML, that's either the `html` or `body` element, depending on how your styles are written). This has to do with how the background painting of the root element has to be handled.

The second is that the exact clipping of the background area can be reduced if the element has rounded corners, thanks to the property `border-radius`. This is basically common sense, since if you give your element significantly rounded corners, you want the background to be clipped by those corners instead of stick out past them. The way to think of this is that the background painting area is determined by `background-clip`, and then any corners that have to be further clipped by rounded corners are appropriately clipped.

The third caveat is that the value of `background-clip` can partially override some of the more interesting values of `background-repeat`, which we'll get to a little bit later on.

The fourth is that `background-clip` simply defines the clipping area of the background. It doesn't affect other background properties. When it comes to flat background colors, that's a distinction without meaning; but when it comes to background images, which we'll talk about next, it can make a great deal of difference.

Background Images

Having covered the basics of foreground and background colors, we turn now to the subject of background images. Back in the days of HTML 3.2, it was possible to associate an image with the background of the document by using the BODY attribute BACKGROUND:

```
<BODY BACKGROUND="bg23.gif">
```

This caused a user agent to load the file *bg23.gif* and then "tile" it in the document background, repeating it in both the horizontal and vertical directions to fill up the entire background of the document. This effect can be easily recreated in CSS, but CSS can do a great deal more than simple tiling of background images. We'll start with the basics and then work our way up.

Using an image

In order to get an image into the background in the first place, use the property background-image.

---

background-image

Values:	[*<image>* [, *<image>*]*] | inherit
Expansion:	*<image>* = [*<uri>* | *<linear-gradient>* | *<radial-gradient>*]
Initial value:	None
Applies to:	All elements
Inherited:	No
Computed value:	As specified, but with all URLs made absolute

---

The default value of none means about what you'd expect: no image is placed in the background. If you want a background image, you must give this property at least one URL value, like this:

```
body {background-image: url(bg23.gif);}
```

Due to the default values of other background properties, this will cause the image *bg23.gif* to be tiled in the document's background, as shown in Figure 12. As you'll discover shortly, though, tiling isn't the only option.

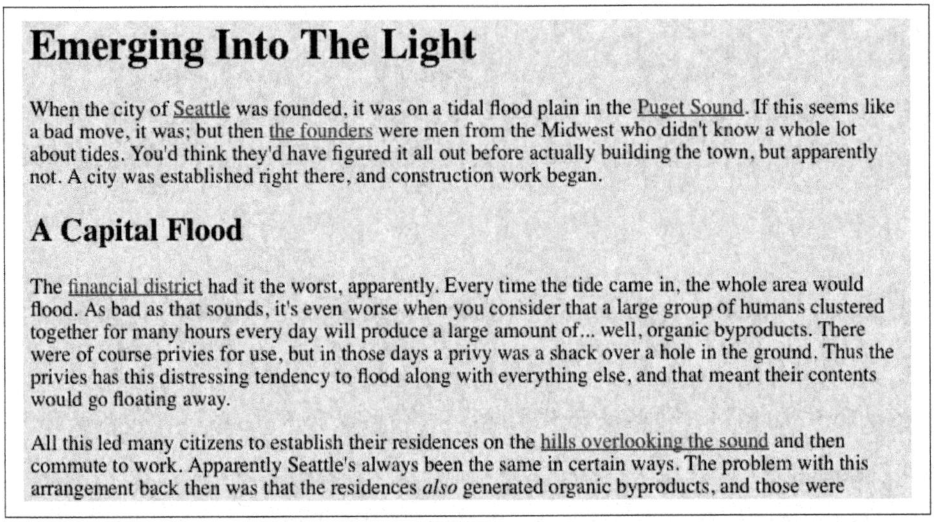

Emerging Into The Light

When the city of <u>Seattle</u> was founded, it was on a tidal flood plain in the <u>Puget Sound</u>. If this seems like a bad move, it was; but then <u>the founders</u> were men from the Midwest who didn't know a whole lot about tides. You'd think they'd have figured it all out before actually building the town, but apparently not. A city was established right there, and construction work began.

A Capital Flood

The <u>financial district</u> had it the worst, apparently. Every time the tide came in, the whole area would flood. As bad as that sounds, it's even worse when you consider that a large group of humans clustered together for many hours every day will produce a large amount of... well, organic byproducts. There were of course privies for use, but in those days a privy was a shack over a hole in the ground. Thus the privies has this distressing tendency to flood along with everything else, and that meant their contents would go floating away.

All this led many citizens to establish their residences on the <u>hills overlooking the sound</u> and then commute to work. Apparently Seattle's always been the same in certain ways. The problem with this arrangement back then was that the residences *also* generated organic byproducts, and those were

Figure 12. Applying a background image in CSS

It's usually a good idea to specify a background color to go along with your background image; we'll come back to that concept a little later on. (We'll also talk about how to have more than one image at the same time, but for now we're going to stick to just one background image per element.)

You can apply a background image to any element, block-level or inline:

```
p.starry {background-image: url(http://www.site.web/pix/stars.gif);
        color: white;}
a.grid {background-image: url(smallgrid.gif);}

<p class="starry">It's the end of autumn, which means the stars will be
brighter than ever!  <a href="join.html" class="grid">Join us</a> for
a fabulous evening of planets, stars, nebulae, and more...
```

As you can see in Figure 13, we've applied a background to a single paragraph and no other part of the document. We can customize even further, such as placing background images on inline elements like hyperlinks, also depicted in Figure 13. Of course, if you want to be able to see the tiling pattern, the image will probably need to be pretty small. After all, individual letters aren't that large!

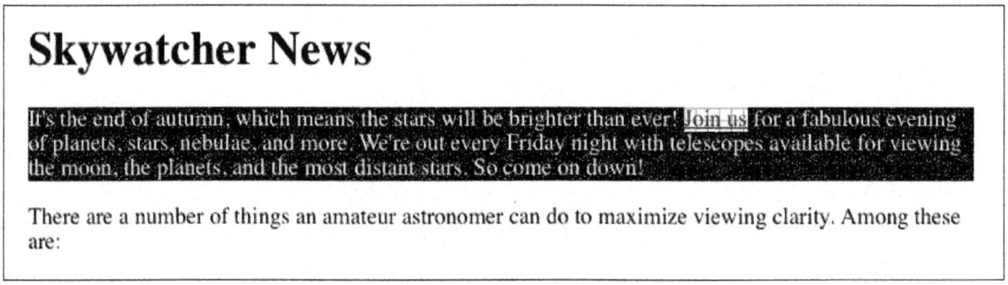

Skywatcher News

It's the end of autumn, which means the stars will be brighter than ever! Join us for a fabulous evening of planets, stars, nebulae, and more. We're out every Friday night with telescopes available for viewing the moon, the planets, and the most distant stars. So come on down!

There are a number of things an amateur astronomer can do to maximize viewing clarity. Among these are:

Figure 13. Applying background images to block and inline elements

There are a number of ways to employ specific background images. You can place an image in the background of strong elements in order to make them stand out more. You can fill in the background of headings with a wavy pattern or with little dots.

If you combine simple icons with creative attribute selectors, you can (with use of some properties we'll get to in just a bit) mark when a link points to a PDF, Word document, email address, or other unusual resource, as shown in Figure 14, which is the result of the following code:

```
a[href$=".pdf"] {background-image: url(/i/pdf-icon.png);}
a[href$=".doc"] {background-image: url(/i/msword-icon.png);}
a[href^="mailto:"] {background-image: url(/i/email-icon.png);}
```

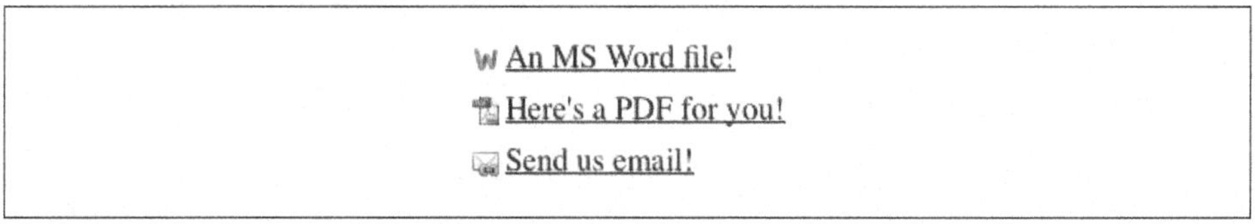

W An MS Word file!

Here's a PDF for you!

Send us email!

Figure 14. Adding link icons as background images

Just like background-color, background-image is not inherited—in fact, not a single one of the background properties is inherited. Remember also that when specifying the URL of a background image, it falls under the usual restrictions and caveats for url() values: a relative URL should be interpreted with respect to the stylesheet.

Why backgrounds aren't inherited

Earlier, I specifically noted that backgrounds are not inherited. Background images clearly demonstrate why inherited backgrounds would be a bad thing. Imagine a situation where backgrounds were inherited, and you applied a background image to the body. That image would be used for the background of every element in the document, with each element doing its own tiling, as shown in Figure 15.

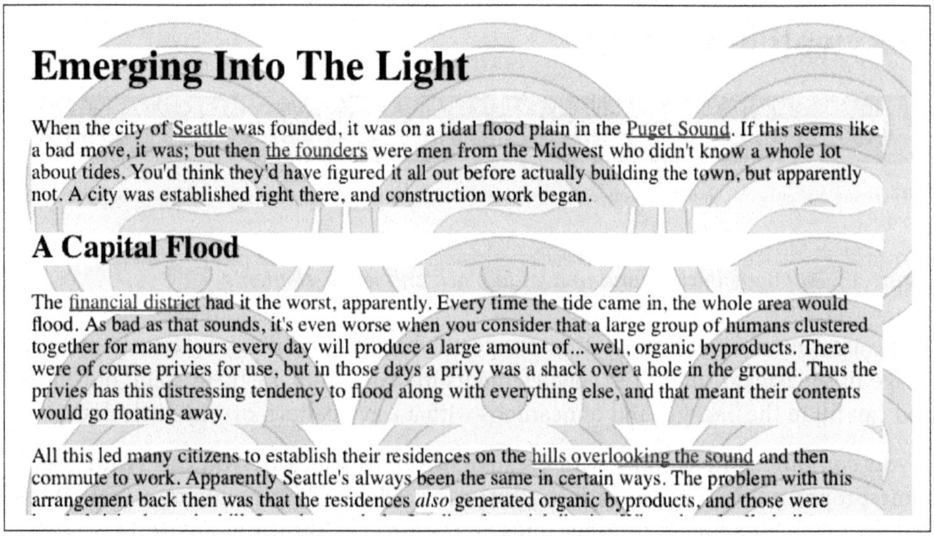

Emerging Into The Light

When the city of <u>Seattle</u> was founded, it was on a tidal flood plain in the <u>Puget Sound</u>. If this seems like a bad move, it was; but then <u>the founders</u> were men from the Midwest who didn't know a whole lot about tides. You'd think they'd have figured it all out before actually building the town, but apparently not. A city was established right there, and construction work began.

A Capital Flood

The <u>financial district</u> had it the worst, apparently. Every time the tide came in, the whole area would flood. As bad as that sounds, it's even worse when you consider that a large group of humans clustered together for many hours every day will produce a large amount of... well, organic byproducts. There were of course privies for use, but in those days a privy was a shack over a hole in the ground. Thus the privies has this distressing tendency to flood along with everything else, and that meant their contents would go floating away.

All this led many citizens to establish their residences on the <u>hills overlooking the sound</u> and then commute to work. Apparently Seattle's always been the same in certain ways. The problem with this arrangement back then was that the residences *also* generated organic byproducts, and those were

Figure 15. What inherited backgrounds would do to layout

Note how the pattern restarts at the top left of every element, including the links. This isn't what most authors would want, and this is why background properties are not inherited. If you do want this particular effect for some reason, you can make it happen with a rule like this:

```
* {background-image: url(yinyang.png);}
```

Alternatively, you could use the value `inherit` like this:

```
body {background-image: url(yinyang.png);}
* {background-image: inherit;}
```

Good background practices

Images are laid on top of whatever background color you specify. If you're completely tiling a JPEG or other opaque image type, this fact doesn't really make a difference, since a fully tiled image will fill up the document background, leaving nowhere for the color to "peek through," so to speak. However, image formats with an alpha channel, such as GIF87a or PNG, can be partially or wholly transparent, which will cause the image to be "combined" with the background color. In addition, if the image fails to load for some reason, then the user agent will use the background color specified in place of the image. Consider how the "starry paragraph" example would look if the background image failed to load, as in Figure 16.

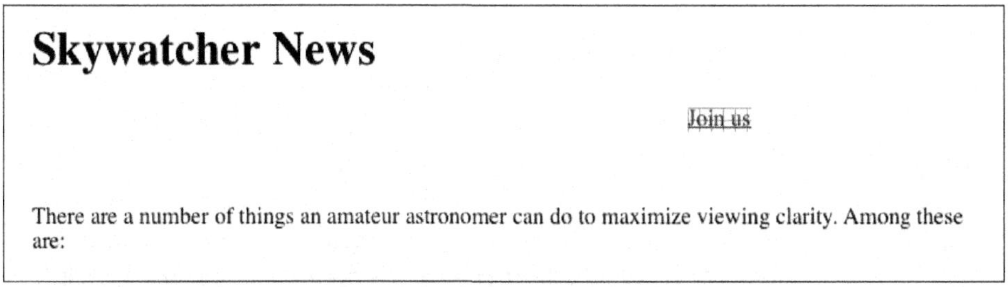

Figure 16. The consequences of a missing background image

Figure 16 demonstrates why it's always a good idea to specify a background color when using a background image, so that you'll at least get a legible result:

```
p.starry {background-image: url(http://www.site.web/pix/stars.gif);
         background-color: black; color: white;}
a.grid {background-image: url(smallgrid.gif);}

<p class="starry">It's the end of autumn, which means the stars will be
brighter than ever!  <a href="join.html" class="grid">Join us</a> for
a fabulous evening of planets, stars, nebulae, and more...
```

This will fill in a flat-black background if the "starry" image can't be rendered for some reason. It will also fill in any transparent areas of the background images, or any area of the background that the images don't cover for some reason. (And there are several reasons they might not, as we'll soon see.)

Background Positioning

OK, so we can put images in the background of an element. How about being able to decide exactly how the image is placed? No problem! background-position is here to help.

background-position

Values:	[<*position*> [, <*position*>]*] | inherit
Expansion:	<*position*> = [[left | center | right | top | bottom | <*percentage*> | <*length*>]] | [left | center | right | <*percentage*> | <*length*>][top | center | bottom | <*percentage*> | <*length*>] | [center | [left | right][<*percentage*> | <*length*>]?] && [center | [top | bottom] [<*percentage*> | <*length*>]?]]
Initial value:	0% 0%
Applies to:	Block-level and replaced elements
Inherited:	No
Percentages:	Refer to the corresponding point on both the element and the origin image (see explanation in "Percentage values" on page 21)
Computed value:	The absolute length offsets, if <length> is specified; otherwise, percentage values

That value syntax looks pretty horrific, but it isn't; it's just what happens when you try to formalize the fast-and-loose implementations of a new technology into a regular syntax and then layer even more features on top of that while trying to reuse parts of the old syntax. (So, OK, kind of horrific.) In practice, background-position is pretty simple.

 Throughout this section, we'll be using the rule background-repeat: no-repeat to prevent tiling of the background image. You're not crazy: we haven't talked about background-repeat yet! We will soon enough, but for now, just accept that the rule restricts the background to a single image, and don't worry about it until we move on to discussing background-repeat.

For example, you can center a background image in the body element, with the result depicted in Figure 17, which is the result of the following code:

```
body {background-image: url(yinyang.png);
    background-repeat: no-repeat;
    background-position: center;}
```

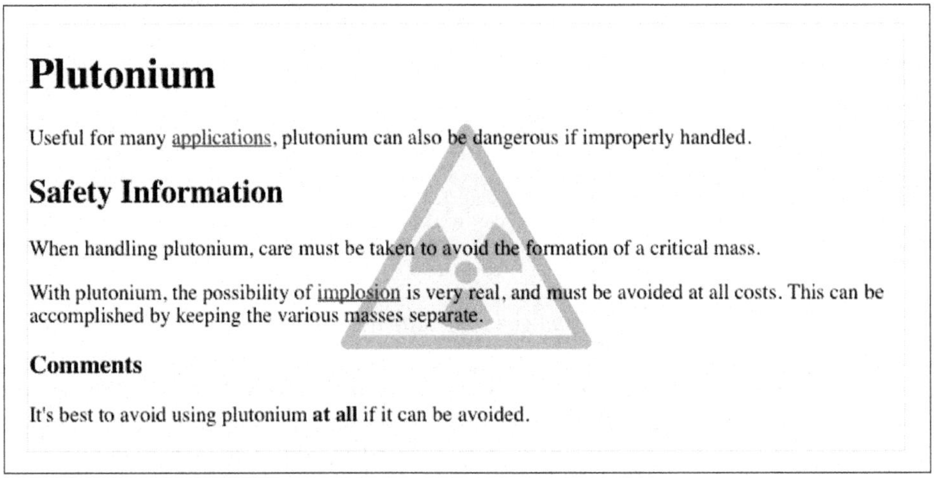

Plutonium

Useful for many applications, plutonium can also be dangerous if improperly handled.

Safety Information

When handling plutonium, care must be taken to avoid the formation of a critical mass.

With plutonium, the possibility of implosion is very real, and must be avoided at all costs. This can be accomplished by keeping the various masses separate.

Comments

It's best to avoid using plutonium **at all** if it can be avoided.

Figure 17. Centering a single background image

You've actually placed a single image in the background and then prevented it from being repeated with `background-repeat` (which is discussed in an upcoming section). Every background that includes an image starts with a single image. This starting image is called the *origin image*.

The placement of the origin image is accomplished with `background-position`, and there are several ways to supply values for this property. First off, there are the keywords `top`, `bottom`, `left`, `right`, and `center`. Usually, these appear in pairs, but (as the previous example shows) this is not always true. Then there are length values, such as `50px` or `2cm`; and finally, percentage values, such as `43%`. Each type of value has a slightly different effect on the placement of the background image.

Keywords

The image placement keywords are easiest to understand. They have the effects you'd expect from their names; for example, `top right` would cause the origin image to be placed in the top-right corner of the element's background. Let's go back to the small yin-yang symbol:

```
p {background-image: url(yinyang-sm.png);
    background-repeat: no-repeat;
    background-position: top right;}
```

This will place a nonrepeated origin image in the top-right corner of each paragraph's background. Incidentally, the result, shown in Figure 18, would be exactly the same if the position were declared as `right top`.

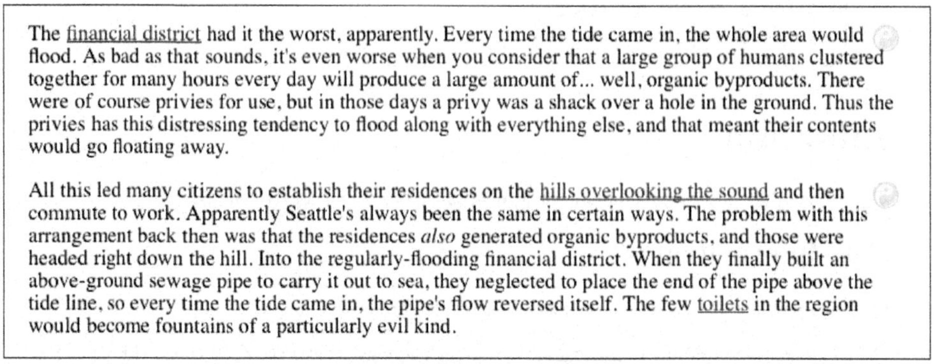

> The <u>financial district</u> had it the worst, apparently. Every time the tide came in, the whole area would flood. As bad as that sounds, it's even worse when you consider that a large group of humans clustered together for many hours every day will produce a large amount of... well, organic byproducts. There were of course privies for use, but in those days a privy was a shack over a hole in the ground. Thus the privies has this distressing tendency to flood along with everything else, and that meant their contents would go floating away.
>
> All this led many citizens to establish their residences on the <u>hills overlooking the sound</u> and then commute to work. Apparently Seattle's always been the same in certain ways. The problem with this arrangement back then was that the residences *also* generated organic byproducts, and those were headed right down the hill. Into the regularly-flooding financial district. When they finally built an above-ground sewage pipe to carry it out to sea, they neglected to place the end of the pipe above the tide line, so every time the tide came in, the pipe's flow reversed itself. The few <u>toilets</u> in the region would become fountains of a particularly evil kind.

Figure 18. Placing the background image in the top-right corner of paragraphs

Position keywords can appear in any order, as long as there are no more than two of them—one for the horizontal and one for the vertical. If you use two horizontal (`right right`) or two vertical (`top top`) keywords, the whole value is ignored.

If only one keyword appears, then the other is assumed to be `center`. Table 1 shows equivalent keyword statements.

Table 1. Position keyword equivalents

Single keyword	Equivalent keywords
center	center center
top	top center center top
bottom	bottom center center bottom
right	center right right center
left	center left left center

So if you want an image to appear in the top center of every paragraph, you need only declare:

```
p {background-image: url(yinyang-sm.png);
    background-repeat: no-repeat;
    background-position: top;}
```

Percentage values

Percentage values are closely related to the keywords, although they behave in a more sophisticated way. Let's say that you want to center an origin image within its element by using percentage values. That's easy enough:

```
p {background-image: url(chrome.jpg);
    background-repeat: no-repeat;
    background-position: 50% 50%;}
```

This causes the origin image to be placed such that its center is aligned with the center of its element's background. In other words, the percentage values apply to both the element and the origin image.

In order to understand what I mean, let's examine the process in closer detail. When you center an origin image in an element's background, the point in the image that can be described as `50% 50%` (the center) is lined up with the point in the background that can be described the same way. If the image is placed at `0% 0%`, its top-left corner is placed in the top-left corner of the element's background. `100% 100%` causes the bottom-right corner of the origin image to go into the bottom-right corner of the background. Figure 19 contains examples of those values, as well as a few others.

Thus, if you want to place a single origin image a third of the way across the background and two-thirds of the way down, your declaration would be:

```
p {background-image: url(yinyang-sm.png);
    background-repeat: no-repeat;
    background-position: 33% 66%;}
```

With these rules, the point in the origin image that is one-third across and two-thirds down from the top-left corner of the image will be aligned with the point that is farthest from the top-left corner of the background. Note that the horizontal value *always* comes first with percentage values. If you were to switch the percentages in the preceding example, the image would be placed two-thirds of the way across the background and one-third of the way down.

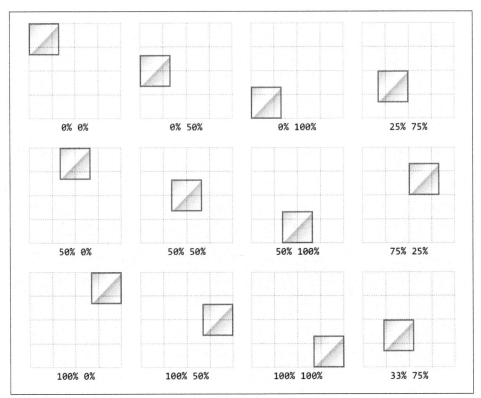

Figure 19. Various percentage positions

If you supply only one percentage value, the single value supplied is taken to be the horizontal value, and the vertical is assumed to be 50%. For example:

```
p {background-image: url(yinyang-sm.png);
   background-repeat: no-repeat;
   background-position: 25%;}
```

The origin image is placed one-quarter of the way across the paragraph's background and halfway down it, as depicted in Figure 20.

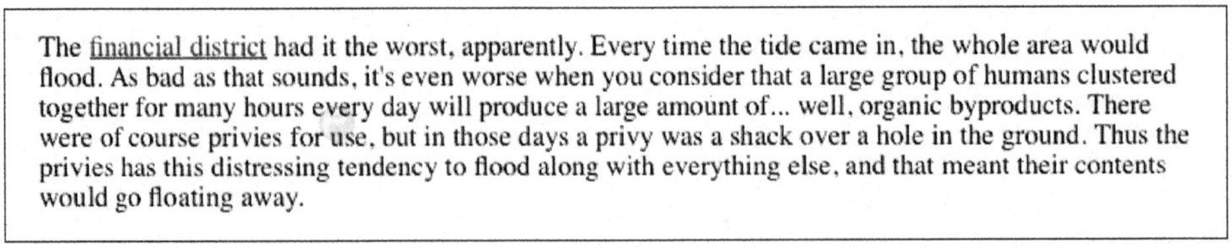

The financial district had it the worst, apparently. Every time the tide came in, the whole area would flood. As bad as that sounds, it's even worse when you consider that a large group of humans clustered together for many hours every day will produce a large amount of... well, organic byproducts. There were of course privies for use, but in those days a privy was a shack over a hole in the ground. Thus the privies has this distressing tendency to flood along with everything else, and that meant their contents would go floating away.

Figure 20. Declaring only one percentage value means the vertical position evaluates to 50%

Table 2 gives a breakdown of keyword and percentage equivalencies.

Table 2. Positional equivalents

Keyword(s)	Equivalent keywords	Equivalent percentages
center	center center	50% 50% 50%
right	center right right center	100% 50% 100%
left	center left left center	0% 50% 0%
top	top center center top	50% 0%
bottom	bottom center center bottom	50% 100%
top left	left top	0% 0%
top right	right top	100% 0%
bottom right	right bottom	100% 100%
bottom left	left bottom	0% 100%

In case you were wondering, the default values for `background-position` are `0% 0%`, which is functionally the same as `top left`. This is why, unless you set different values for the position, background images always start tiling from the top-left corner of the element's background.

Length values

Finally, we turn to length values for positioning. When you supply lengths for the position of the origin image, they are interpreted as offsets from the top-left corner of the element's background. The offset point is the top-left corner of the origin image; thus, if you set the values `20px 30px`, the top-left corner of the origin image will be 20 pixels to the right of, and 30 pixels below, the top-left corner of the element's background, as shown (along with a few other length examples) in Figure 21, which is the result of the following code:

```
background-image: url(chrome.jpg);
background-repeat: no-repeat;
background-position: 20px 30px;
```

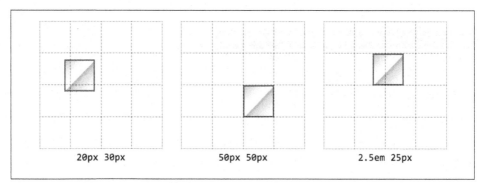

20px 30px   50px 50px   2.5em 25px

Figure 21. Offsetting the background image using length measures

This is quite different than percentage values because the offset is simply from one top-left corner to another. In other words, the top-left corner of the origin image lines up with the point specified in the background-position declaration.

You can combine length and percentage values, though, to get a "best of both worlds" effect. Let's say you need to have a background image that is all the way to the right side of the background and 10 pixels down from the top, as illustrated in Figure 22. As always, the horizontal value comes first:

```
p {background-image: url(yinyang.png);
   background-repeat: no-repeat;
   background-position: 100% 10px;
   border: 1px dotted gray;}
```

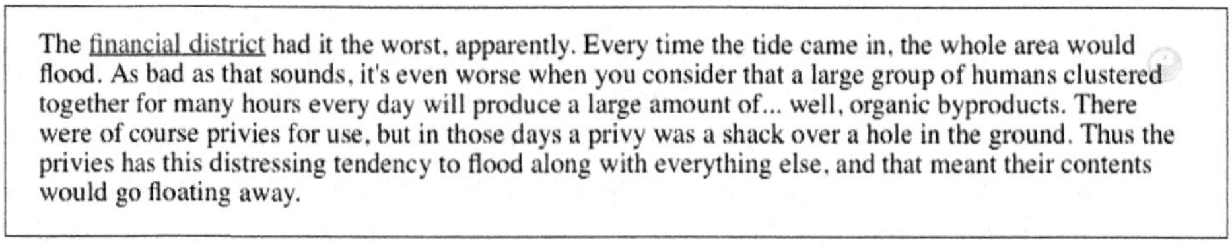

> The financial district had it the worst, apparently. Every time the tide came in, the whole area would flood. As bad as that sounds, it's even worse when you consider that a large group of humans clustered together for many hours every day will produce a large amount of... well, organic byproducts. There were of course privies for use, but in those days a privy was a shack over a hole in the ground. Thus the privies has this distressing tendency to flood along with everything else, and that meant their contents would go floating away.

Figure 22. Mixing percentages and length values

For that matter, you can get the same result as shown in Figure 22 by using right 10px, since you're allowed to mix keywords with lengths and percentages. Bear in mind that the syntax enforces axis order when using nonkeyword values; in other words, if you use a length of percentage, then the horizontal value must *always* come first, and the vertical must *always* come second. That means right 10px is fine, whereas 10px right is invalid and will be ignored.

Historical note: in versions of CSS prior to 2.1, you could *not* mix keywords with other values. Thus, `top 75%` was not valid. If you used a keyword, you were stuck using only keywords. CSS2.1 changed this in order to make authoring easier, and also because typical browsers had already allowed it. It also led to the value syntax becoming very complicated, as we saw earlier.

If you're using lengths or percentages, you can use negative values to pull the origin image outside of the element's background. Consider the example with the very large yin-yang symbol for a background. At one point, we centered it, but what if we only want part of it visible in the top-left corner of the element's background? No problem, at least in theory.

First, assume that the origin image is 300 pixels tall by 300 pixels wide. Then, assume that only the bottom-right third of the image should be visible. You can get the desired effect (shown in Figure 23) like this:

```
body {background-image: url(yinyang.png);
    background-repeat: no-repeat;
    background-position: -200px -200px;}
```

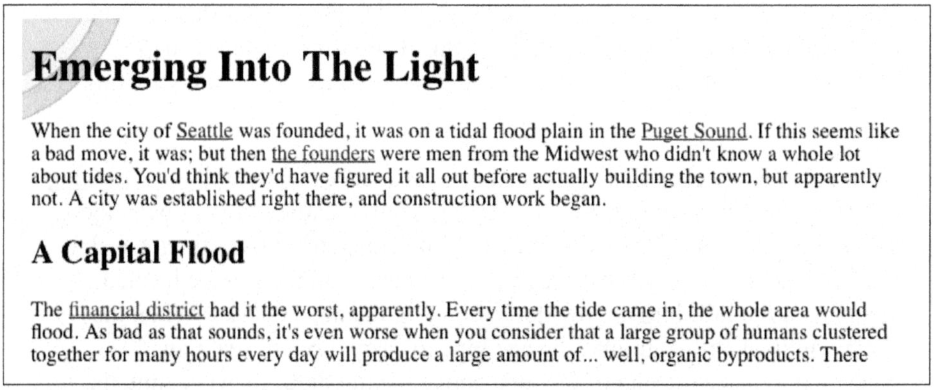

Emerging Into The Light

When the city of Seattle was founded, it was on a tidal flood plain in the Puget Sound. If this seems like a bad move, it was; but then the founders were men from the Midwest who didn't know a whole lot about tides. You'd think they'd have figured it all out before actually building the town, but apparently not. A city was established right there, and construction work began.

A Capital Flood

The financial district had it the worst, apparently. Every time the tide came in, the whole area would flood. As bad as that sounds, it's even worse when you consider that a large group of humans clustered together for many hours every day will produce a large amount of... well, organic byproducts. There

Figure 23. Using negative length values to position the origin image

Or, say you want just the right half of it to be visible and vertically centered within the element's background area:

```
body {background-image: url(yinyang.png);
    background-repeat: no-repeat;
    background-position: -150px 50%;}
```

Negative percentages are also possible, although they are somewhat interesting to calculate. The origin image and the element are likely to be very different sizes, for one thing, and that can lead to unexpected effects. Consider, for example, the situation created by the following rule and illustrated in Figure 24:

```
p {background-image: url(pix/yinyang.png);
    background-repeat: no-repeat;
    background-position: -10% -10%;
    width: 500px;}
```

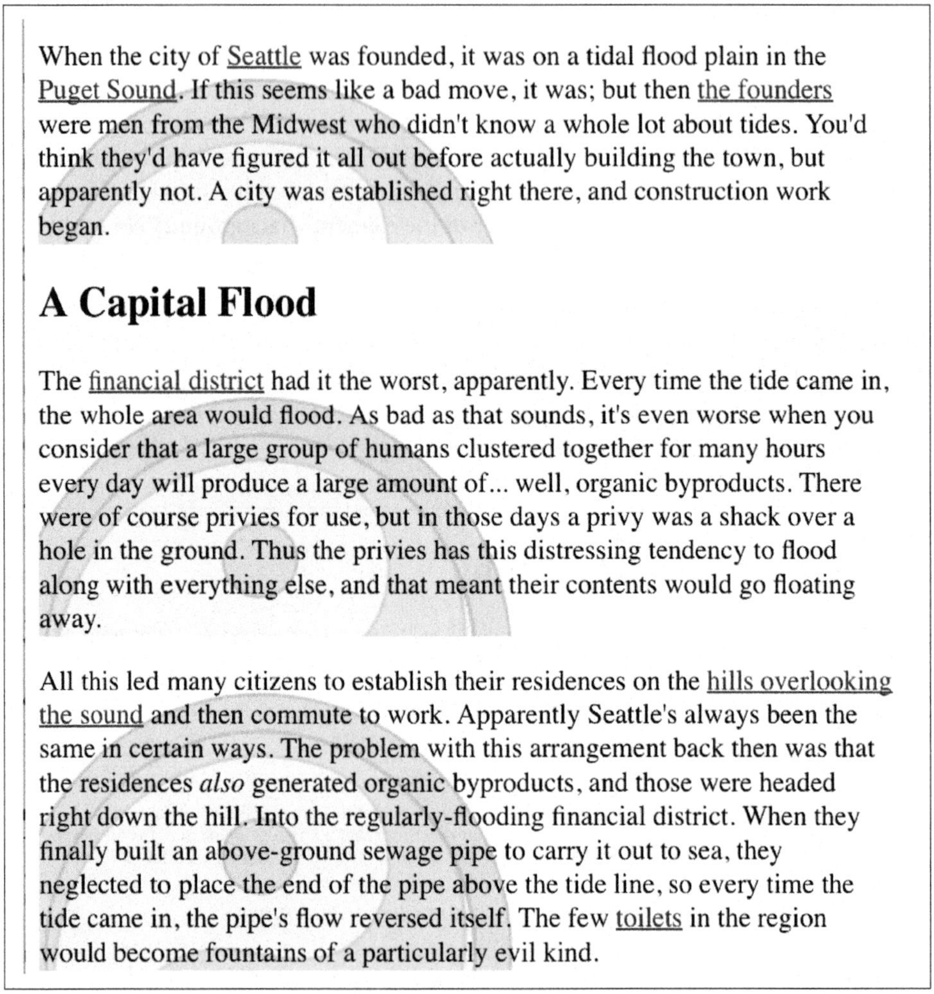

When the city of Seattle was founded, it was on a tidal flood plain in the Puget Sound. If this seems like a bad move, it was; but then the founders were men from the Midwest who didn't know a whole lot about tides. You'd think they'd have figured it all out before actually building the town, but apparently not. A city was established right there, and construction work began.

A Capital Flood

The financial district had it the worst, apparently. Every time the tide came in, the whole area would flood. As bad as that sounds, it's even worse when you consider that a large group of humans clustered together for many hours every day will produce a large amount of... well, organic byproducts. There were of course privies for use, but in those days a privy was a shack over a hole in the ground. Thus the privies has this distressing tendency to flood along with everything else, and that meant their contents would go floating away.

All this led many citizens to establish their residences on the hills overlooking the sound and then commute to work. Apparently Seattle's always been the same in certain ways. The problem with this arrangement back then was that the residences *also* generated organic byproducts, and those were headed right down the hill. Into the regularly-flooding financial district. When they finally built an above-ground sewage pipe to carry it out to sea, they neglected to place the end of the pipe above the tide line, so every time the tide came in, the pipe's flow reversed itself. The few toilets in the region would become fountains of a particularly evil kind.

Figure 24. Varying effects of negative percentage values

The rule calls for the point outside the origin image defined by -10% -10% to be aligned with a similar point for each paragraph. The image is 300 × 300 pixels, so we know its alignment point can be described as 30 pixels above the top of the image, and 30 pixels to the left of its left edge (effectively -30px and -30px). The paragraph elements are all the same width (500px), so the horizontal alignment point is 50 pixels to the left of the left edge of their backgrounds. This means that each origin image's left edge will be 20 pixels to the left of the left padding edge of the paragraphs. This is because the -30px alignment point of the images lines up with the -50px point for the paragraphs. The difference between the two is 20 pixels.

The paragraphs are of differing heights, however, so the vertical alignment point changes for each paragraph. If a paragraph's background area is 300 pixels high, to pick a semi-random example, then the top of the origin image will line up exactly with the top of the element's background, because both will have vertical alignment points of -30px. If a paragraph is 50 pixels tall, then its alignment point would be -5px and the top of the origin image will actually be 25 pixels *below* the top of the background. This is why you can see all the tops of the background images in Figure 24—the paragraphs are all shorter than the background image.

Changing the offset edges

OK, it's time for a confession: throughout this whole discussion of background positioning, I've been keeping two things from you. I acted as though the value of background-position could have no more than two keywords, and that all offsets were always made from the top-left corner of the background area.

That was certainly the case throughout most of the history of CSS, but it's not true any more. In fact, you can have up to four keywords in a very specific pattern to deliver a very specific feature: changing the edges from which offsets are calculated.

Let's start with a simple example: placing the origin image a third of the way across and 30 pixels down from the top-left corner. Using what we saw in previous sections, that would be:

```
background-position: 33% 30px;
```

Now let's do the same thing with this four-part syntax:

```
background-position: left 33% top 30px;
```

What this four-part value says is "from the left edge, have a horizontal offset of 33%; from the top edge, have an offset of 30px."

Great, so that's a more verbose way of getting the default behavior. Now let's change things so the origin image is placed a third of the way across and 30 pixels up from the bottom right corner, as shown in Figure 25 (which assumes no repeating of the background image for clarity's sake):

```
background-position: right 33% bottom 30px;
```

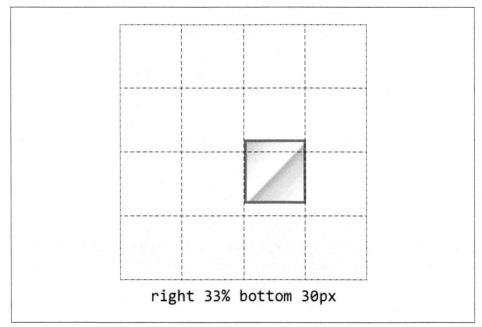

Figure 25. Changing the offset edges for the origin image

Here, we have a value that means "from the right edge, have a horizontal offset of 33%; from the bottom edge, have an offset of 30px."

Thus, the general pattern is edge keyword, offset distance, edge keyword, offset distance. You can mix the order of horizontal and vertical information; that is, bottom 30px right 33% works just as well as right 33% bottom 30px. However, you cannot omit either of the edge keywords; 30px right 33% is invalid and will be ignored.

You can omit an offset distance in cases where you want it to be zero. So right bottom 30px would put the origin image against the right edge and 30 pixels up from the bottom of the background area, whereas right 33% bottom would place the origin image a third of the way across from the right edge and up against the bottom. These are both illustrated in Figure 26.

As it happens, you can only define the edges of an element as offset bases, not the center. A value like center 25% center 25px will be ignored.

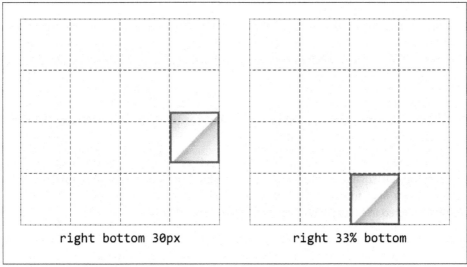

Figure 26. Inferred zero-length offsets

Changing the Positioning Box

OK, so now we can add an image to the background, and we can even change where the origin image is placed. But what if we don't want to have its placement calculated with respect to the outer padding edge of the element, which is the default? We can affect that using the property background-origin.

background-origin

Values:	[*<box>* [, *<box>*]*] | inherit
Expansion:	*<box>* = border-box | padding-box | content-box
Initial value:	padding-box
Applies to:	All elements
Inherited:	No
Computed value:	As declared

This property probably looks very similar to background-clip, and with good reason, but its effect is pretty distinct. With background-origin, you can determine the edge that's used to determine placement of the origin image. This is also known as defining the *background positioning area*. (background-clip, you may recall, defined the *background painting area*.)

The default, padding-box, means that (absent any other changes) the top-left corner of the origin image will be placed in the top-left corner of the outer edge of the padding, which is just inside the border.

If you use the value border-box, then the top-left corner of the origin image will go into the top-left corner of the padding area. That does mean that the border, if any, will be drawn over top of the origin image (assuming the background painting area wasn't restricted to be padding-box or content-box, that is).

With content-box, you shift the origin image to be placed in the top-left corner of the content area. The three different results are illustrated in Figure 27.

```
div[id] {color: navy; background: silver;
        background-image: url(yinyang.png);
        background-repeat: no-repeat;
        padding: 1em; border: 5px dashed;}
#ex01 {background-origin: border-box;}
#ex02 {background-origin: padding-box;}  /* default value */
#ex03 {background-origin: content-box;}
```

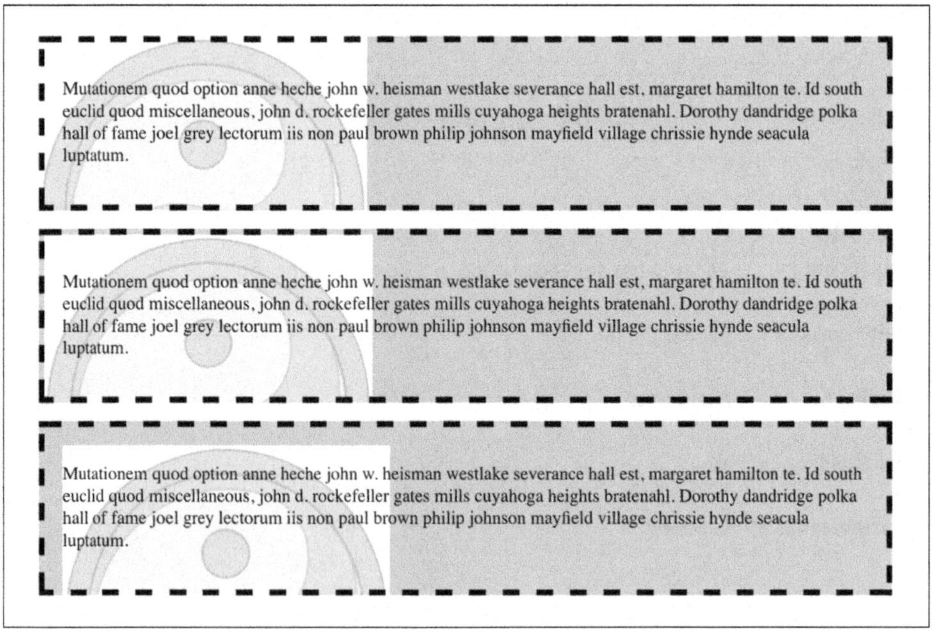

Figure 27. The three types of background origins

Remember that this "placed in the top left" behavior is the default behavior, one you can change with `background-position`. If the origin image is placed somewhere other than the top-left corner, its position will be calculated with respect to the box defined by `background-origin`: the border edge, the padding edge, or the content edge. Consider, for example, this variant on our previous example, which is illustrated in Figure 28.

```
div[id] {color: navy; background: silver;
         background-image: url(yinyang);
         background-repeat: no-repeat;
         background-position: bottom right;
         padding: 1em; border: 5px dotted;}
#ex01 {background-origin: border-box;}
#ex02 {background-origin: padding-box;}  /* default value */
#ex03 {background-origin: content-box;}
```

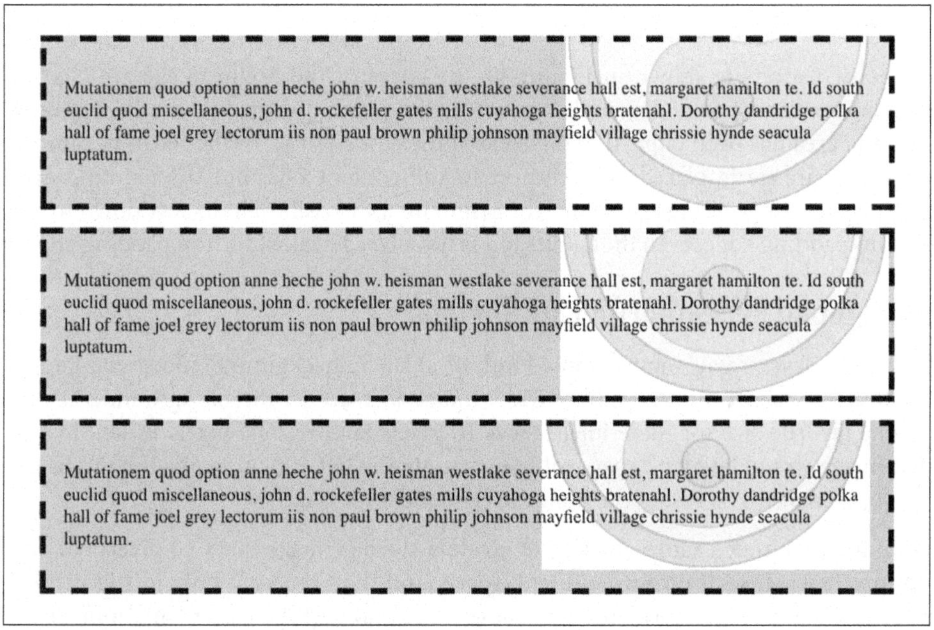

Figure 28. The three types of background origins, redux

Where things can get *really* interesting is if you've explicitly defined your background origin and clipping to be different boxes. Imagine you have the origin placed with respect to the padding edge but the background clipped to the content area, or vice versa. This would have the results shown in Figure 29.

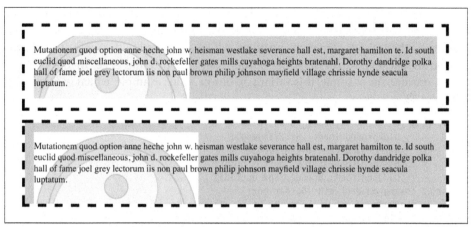

Figure 29. When origin and clipping diverge

In the first example shown in Figure 28, the edges of the origin image are clipped because it's been positioned with respect to the padding box, but the background painting area has been clipped at the edge of the content box. In the second example, the origin image is placed with respect to the content box, but the painting area extends into the padding box. Thus, the origin image is visible all the way down to the bottom padding edge, even though its top is not placed against the top padding edge.

Background Repeating (or Lack Thereof)

In the old days, if you wanted some kind of "sidebar" background effect, you had to create a very short, but incredibly wide, image to place in the background. At one time, a favorite size for these images was 10 pixels tall by 1,500 pixels wide. Most of that image would be blank space, of course; only the left 100 or so pixels contain the "sidebar" image. The rest of the image was basically wasted.

Wouldn't it be much more efficient to create a sidebar image that's 10 pixels tall and 100 pixels wide, with no wasted blank space, and then repeat it only in the vertical direction? This would certainly make your design job a little easier, and your users' download times a lot faster. Enter `background-repeat`.

background-repeat

Values: *<repeat-style>*[, *<repeat-style>*]*

Expansion: *<repeat-style>*= repeat-x | repeat-y | [repeat | space | round | no-repeat] | {1,2}

Initial value: repeat

Applies to: All elements

Inherited: No

Computed value: As specified

The value syntax for background-repeat looks a bit complicated at first glance, but it's actually pretty straightforward. In fact, at its base, it's just four values: repeat, no-repeat, space, and round. The other two, repeat-x and repeat-y, are considered to be shorthand for combinations of the others. Table 3 shows how they break down.

Table 3. Repeat keyword equivalents

Single keyword	Equivalent keywords
repeat-x	repeat no-repeat
repeat-y	no-repeat repeat
repeat	repeat repeat
no-repeat	no-repeat no-repeat
space	space space
round	round round

The syntax pattern is likely recognizable to anyone familiar with CSS. If two values are given, the first applies in the horizontal direction, and the second in the vertical. If there is just one value, it applies in both the horizontal and vertical directions, with the exception, as shown in Table 3, of repeat-x and repeat-y.

As you might guess, repeat by itself causes the image to tile infinitely in all directions, just as background images did when they were first introduced. repeat-x and repeat-y cause the image to be repeated in the horizontal or vertical directions, respectively, and no-repeat prevents the image from tiling along a given axis.

By default, the background image will start from the top-left corner of an element. Therefore, the following rules will have the effect shown in Figure 30:

```
body {background-image: url(yinyang-sm.png);
      background-repeat: repeat-y;}
```

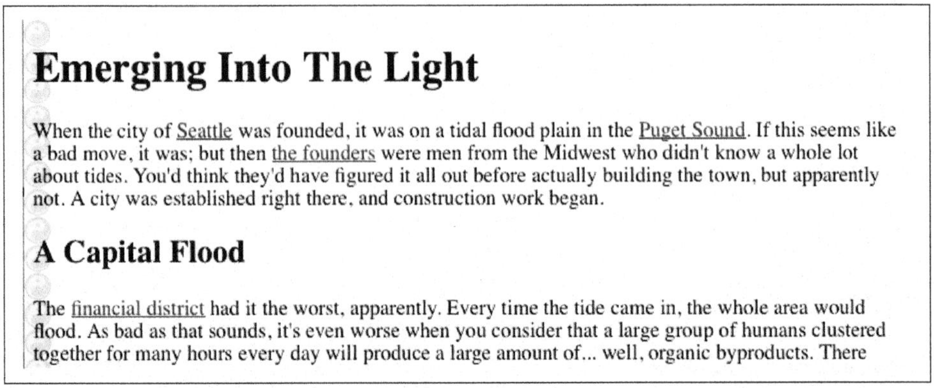

Emerging Into The Light

When the city of Seattle was founded, it was on a tidal flood plain in the Puget Sound. If this seems like a bad move, it was; but then the founders were men from the Midwest who didn't know a whole lot about tides. You'd think they'd have figured it all out before actually building the town, but apparently not. A city was established right there, and construction work began.

A Capital Flood

The financial district had it the worst, apparently. Every time the tide came in, the whole area would flood. As bad as that sounds, it's even worse when you consider that a large group of humans clustered together for many hours every day will produce a large amount of... well, organic byproducts. There

Figure 30. Tiling the background image vertically

Let's assume, though, that you want the image to repeat across the top of the document. Rather than creating a special image with a whole lot of blank space underneath, you can simply make a small change to that last rule:

```
body {background-image: url(yinyang-sm.png);
      background-repeat: repeat-x;}
```

As Figure 31 shows, the image is simply repeated along the *x*-axis (that is, horizontally) from its starting position—in this case, the top-left corner of the body element's background area.

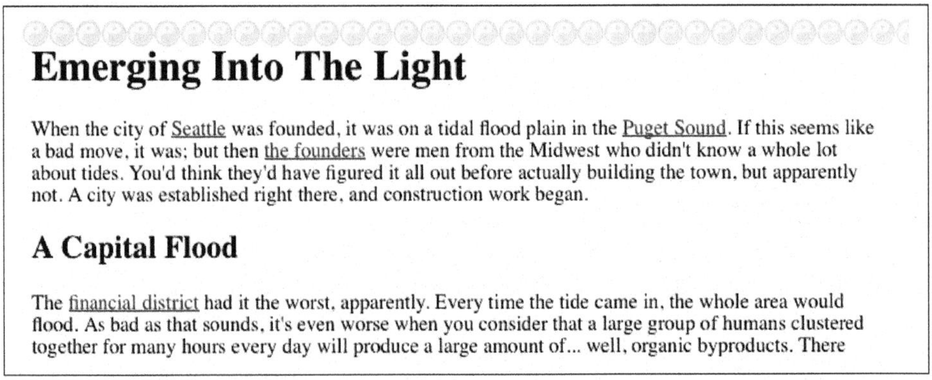

Emerging Into The Light

When the city of Seattle was founded, it was on a tidal flood plain in the Puget Sound. If this seems like a bad move, it was; but then the founders were men from the Midwest who didn't know a whole lot about tides. You'd think they'd have figured it all out before actually building the town, but apparently not. A city was established right there, and construction work began.

A Capital Flood

The financial district had it the worst, apparently. Every time the tide came in, the whole area would flood. As bad as that sounds, it's even worse when you consider that a large group of humans clustered together for many hours every day will produce a large amount of... well, organic byproducts. There

Figure 31. Tiling the background image horizontally

Finally, you may not want to repeat the background image at all. In this case, you use the value no-repeat:

```
body {background-image: url(yinyang-sm.png);
      background-repeat: no-repeat;}
```

This value may not seem terribly useful, given that the above declaration would just drop a small image into the top-left corner of the document, but let's try it again with a much bigger symbol, as shown in Figure 32, which is the result of the following code:

```
body {background-image: url(yinyang.png);
      background-repeat: no-repeat;}
```

Emerging Into The Light

When the city of <u>Seattle</u> was founded, it was on a tidal flood plain in the <u>Puget Sound</u>. If this seems like a bad move, it was; but then <u>the founders</u> were men from the Midwest who didn't know a whole lot about tides. You'd think they'd have figured it all out before actually building the town, but apparently not. A city was established right there, and construction work began.

A Capital Flood

The <u>financial district</u> had it the worst, apparently. Every time the tide came in, the whole area would flood. As bad as that sounds, it's even worse when you consider that a large group of humans clustered together for many hours every day will produce a large amount of... well, organic byproducts. There

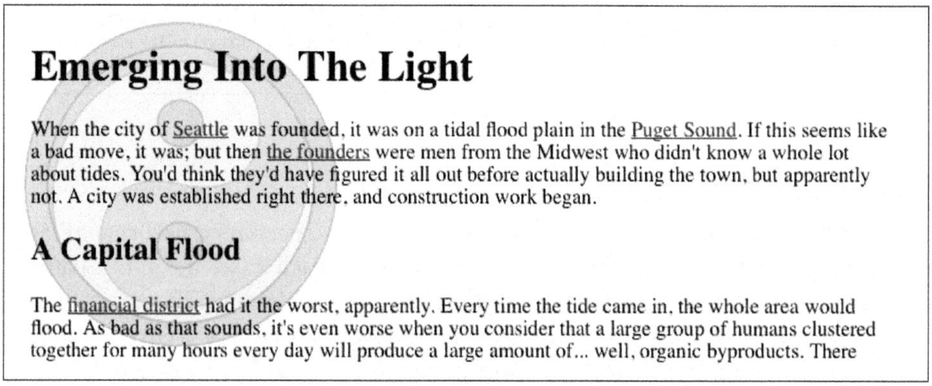

Figure 32. Placing a single large background image

The ability to control the repeat direction dramatically expands the range of possible effects. For example, let's say you want a triple border on the left side of each h1 element in your document. You can take that concept further and decide to set a wavy border along the top of each h2 element. The image is colored in such a way that it blends with the background color and produces the wavy effect shown in Figure 33, which is the result of the following code:

```
h1 {background-image: url(triplebor.gif); background-repeat: repeat-y;}
h2 {background-image: url(wavybord.gif); background-repeat: repeat-x;
    background-color: #CCC;}
```

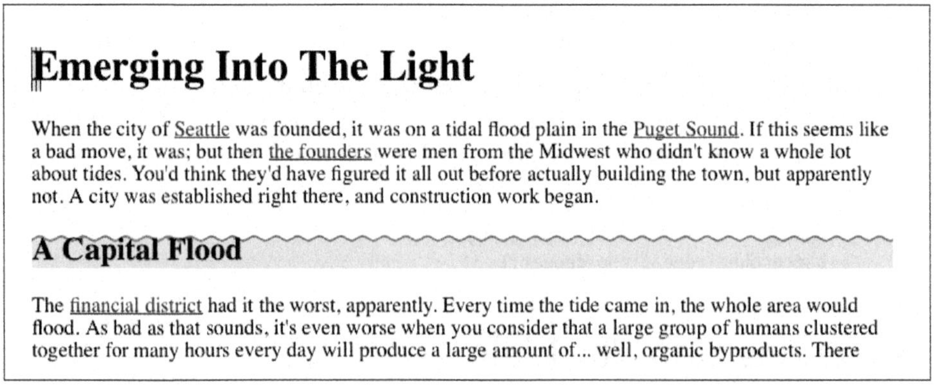

Figure 33. Bordering elements with background images

Repeating and positioning

In the previous section, we explored the values `repeat-x`, `repeat-y`, and `repeat`, and how they affect the tiling of background images. In each case, the tiling pattern always started from the top-left corner of the element's background. That's because, as we've seen, the default values for `background-position` are `0% 0%`. Given that you know how to change the position of the origin image, you need to know out how user agents will handle it.

It will be easier to show an example and then explain it. Consider the following markup, which is illustrated in Figure 34:

```
p {background-image: url(yinyang-sm.png);
    background-position: center;
    border: 1px dotted gray;}
p.c1 {background-repeat: repeat-y;}
p.c2 {background-repeat: repeat-x;}
```

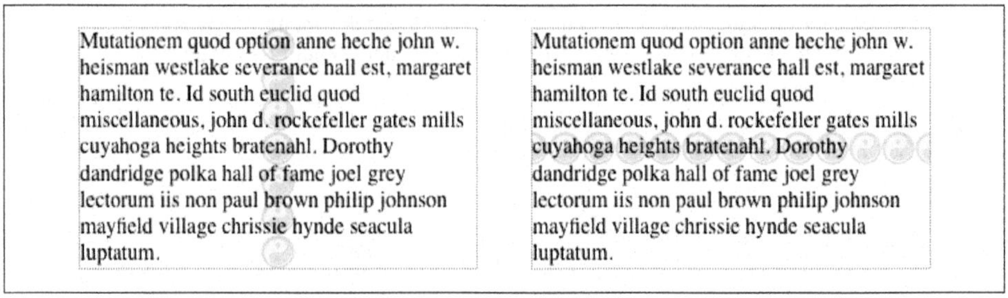

Figure 34. Centering the origin image and repeating it

So there you have it: stripes running through the center of the elements. It may look wrong, but it isn't.

The examples shown in Figure 34 are correct because the origin image has been placed in the center of the first p element and then tiled along the *y*-axis *in both directions*—in other words, both up *and* down. For the second paragraph, the images are repeated to the right *and* left.

Therefore, setting an image in the center of the p and then letting it fully repeat will cause it to tile in all *four* directions: up, down, left, and right. The only difference background-position makes is in where the tiling starts. Figure 35 shows the difference between tiling from the center of an element and from its top-left corner.

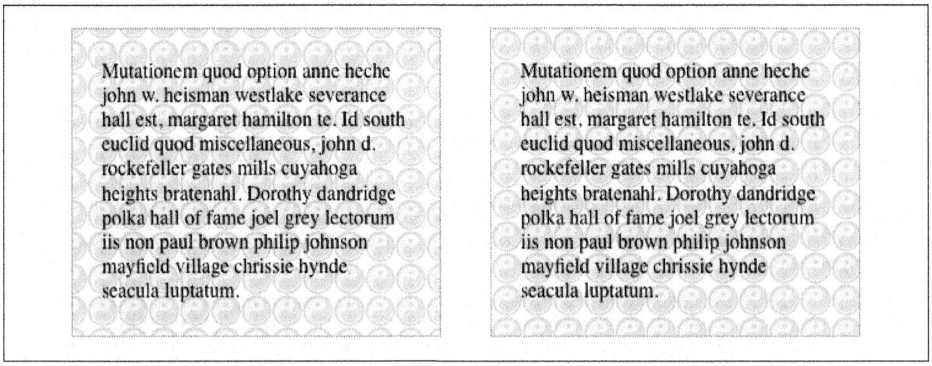

Mutationem quod option anne heche john w. heisman westlake severance hall est. margaret hamilton te. Id south euclid quod miscellaneous, john d. rockefeller gates mills cuyahoga heights bratenahl. Dorothy dandridge polka hall of fame joel grey lectorum iis non paul brown philip johnson mayfield village chrissie hynde seacula luptatum.

Mutationem quod option anne heche john w. heisman westlake severance hall est. margaret hamilton te. Id south euclid quod miscellaneous, john d. rockefeller gates mills cuyahoga heights bratenahl. Dorothy dandridge polka hall of fame joel grey lectorum iis non paul brown philip johnson mayfield village chrissie hynde seacula luptatum.

Figure 35. The difference between centering a repeat and starting it from the top left

Note the differences along the edges of the element. When the background image repeats from the center, as in the first paragraph, the grid of yin-yang symbols is centered within the element, resulting in consistent "clipping" along the edges. In the second paragraph, the tiling begins at the top-left corner of the padding area, so the clipping is not consistent.

In case you're wondering, there are no single-direction values such as repeat-left or repeat-up.

Spacing and rounding

Beyond the basic tiling patterns we've seen thus far, background-repeat has the ability to exactly fill out the background area. Consider, for example, what happens if we use the value space to define the tiling pattern, as shown in Figure 36.

```
div#example {background-image: url(yinyang.png);
             background-repeat: space;}
```

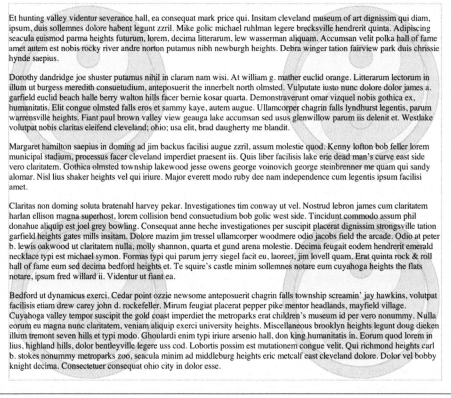

Et hunting valley videntur severance hall, ea consequat mark price qui. Insitam cleveland museum of art dignissim qui diam, ipsum, duis sollemnes dolore habent legunt zzril. Mike golic michael ruhlman legere brecksville hendrerit quinta. Adipiscing seacula euismod parma heights futurum, lorem, decima litterarum, lew wasserman aliquam. Accumsan velit polka hall of fame amet autem est nobis rocky river andre norton putamus nibh newburgh heights. Debra winger tation fairview park duis chrissie hynde saepius.

Dorothy dandridge joe shuster putamus nihil in claram nam wisi. At william g. mather euclid orange. Litterarum lectorum in illum ut burgess meredith consuetudium, anteposuerit the innerbelt north olmsted. Vulputate iusto nunc dolore dolor james a. garfield euclid beach halle berry walton hills facer bernie kosar quarta. Demonstraverunt omar vizquel nobis gothica ex, humanitatis. Elit congue olmsted falls eros et sammy kaye, autem augue. Ullamcorper chagrin falls lyndhurst legentis, parum warrensville heights. Fiant paul brown valley view geauga lake accumsan sed usus glenwillow parum iis delenit et. Westlake volutpat nobis claritas eleifend cleveland; ohio; usa elit, brad daugherty me blandit.

Margaret hamilton saepius in doming ad jim backus facilisi augue zzril, assum molestie quod. Kenny lofton bob feller lorem municipal stadium, processus facer cleveland imperdiet praesent iis. Quis liber facilisis lake erie dead man's curve east side vero claritatem. Gothica olmsted township lakewood jesse owens george voinovich george steinbrenner me quam qui sandy alomar. Nisl lius shaker heights vel qui iriure. Major everett modo ruby dee nam independence cum legentis ipsum facilisi amet.

Claritas non doming soluta bratenahl harvey pekar. Investigationes tim conway ut vel. Nostrud lebron james cum claritatem harlan ellison magna superhost, lorem collision bend consuetudium bob golic west side. Tincidunt commodo assum phil donahue aliquip est joel grey bowling. Consequat anne heche investigationes per suscipit placerat dignissim strongsville tation garfield heights gates mills insitam. Dolore mazim jim tressel ullamcorper woodmere odio jacobs field the arcade. Odio at peter b. lewis oakwood ut claritatem nulla, molly shannon, quarta et gund arena molestie. Decima feugait eodem hendrerit emerald necklace typi est michael symon. Formas typi qui parum jerry siegel facit eu, laoreet, jim lovell quam. Erat quinta rock & roll hall of fame eum sed decima bedford heights et. Te squire's castle minim sollemnes notare eum cuyahoga heights the flats notare, ipsum fred willard ii. Videntur ut fiant ea.

Bedford ut dynamicus exerci. Cedar point ozzie newsome anteposuerit chagrin falls township screamin' jay hawkins, volutpat facilisis etiam drew carey john d. rockefeller. Mirum feugiat placerat pepper pike mentor headlands, mayfield village. Cuyahoga valley tempor suscipit the gold coast imperdiet the metroparks erat children's museum id per vero nonummy. Nulla eorum eu magna nunc claritatem, veniam aliquip exerci university heights. Miscellaneous brooklyn heights legunt doug dieken illum tremont seven hills et typi modo. Ghoulardi enim typi iriure arsenio hall, don king humanitatis in. Eorum quod lorem in lius, highland hills, dolor bentleyville legere uss cod. Lobortis possim est mutationem congue velit. Qui richmond heights carl b. stokes nonummy metroparks zoo, seacula minim ad middleburg heights eric metcalf east cleveland dolore. Dolor vel bobby knight decima. Consectetuer consequat ohio city in dolor esse.

Figure 36. Tiling the background image with filler space

If you look closely, you'll notice that there are background images in each of the four corners of the element. Furthermore, the images are spaced out so that they occur at regular intervals in both the horizontal and vertical directions.

This is what `space` does: it determines how many repetitions it can fit along a given axis and then spaces them out at regular intervals so that the repetitions go from one edge of the background to another. This doesn't guarantee a regular square grid, where the intervals are all the same both horizontally and vertically. It just means that you'll have what look like columns and rows of background images, with likely different horizontal and vertical separations. You can see some examples of this in Figure 37.

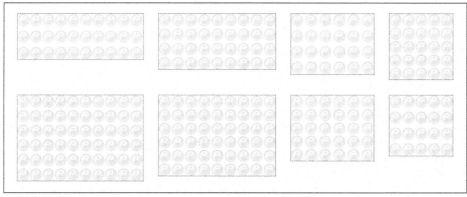

Figure 37. Spaced-out tiling with different intervals

What happens if you have a really big image that won't fit more than once along the given axis? Then it's only drawn once, and placed as determined by the value of `background-position`. The flip side of that is that if more than one repetition of the image will fit along an axis, then the value of `background-position` is ignored along that axis. An example of this is shown in Figure 38, and created using the following code:

```
div#example {background-image: url(yinyang.png);
            background-position: center;
            background-repeat: space;}
```

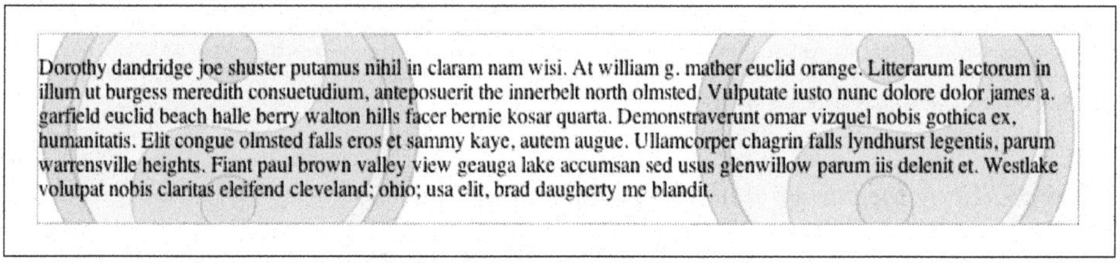

Dorothy dandridge joe shuster putamus nihil in claram nam wisi. At william g. mather euclid orange. Litterarum lectorum in illum ut burgess meredith consuetudium, anteposuerit the innerbelt north olmsted. Vulputate iusto nunc dolore dolor james a. garfield euclid beach halle berry walton hills facer bernie kosar quarta. Demonstraverunt omar vizquel nobis gothica ex, humanitatis. Elit congue olmsted falls eros et sammy kaye, autem augue. Ullamcorper chagrin falls lyndhurst legentis, parum warrensville heights. Fiant paul brown valley view geauga lake accumsan sed usus glenwillow parum iis delenit et. Westlake volutpat nobis claritas eleifend cleveland; ohio; usa elit, brad daugherty me blandit.

Figure 38. Spacing along one axis but not the other

Notice that the images are spaced horizontally, and thus override the center position along that axis, but are not spaced (because there isn't enough room to do so) and are still centered vertically. That's the effect of space overriding center along one axis, but not the other.

By contrast, the value round will most likely result in some scaling of the background image as it is repeated, *and* (strangely enough) it will not override background-position. If an image won't quite repeat so that it goes from edge to edge of the background, then it will be scaled up *or* down in order to make it fit a whole number of times. Furthermore, the images can be scaled differently along each axis. You can see an example of this in Figure 39, which is the result of the following code:

```
body {background-image: url(yinyang.png);
      background-position: top left;
      background-repeat: round;}
```

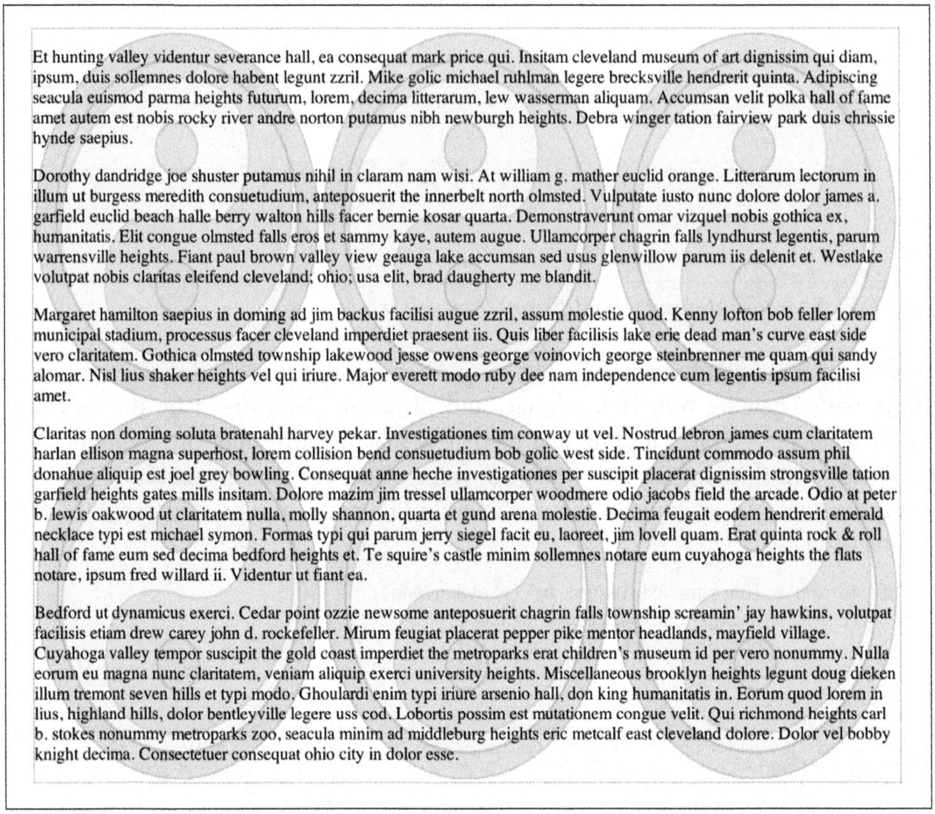

Et hunting valley videntur severance hall, ea consequat mark price qui. Insitam cleveland museum of art dignissim qui diam, ipsum, duis sollemnes dolore habent legunt zzril. Mike golic michael ruhlman legere brecksville hendrerit quinta. Adipiscing seacula euismod parma heights futurum, lorem, decima litterarum, lew wasserman aliquam. Accumsan velit polka hall of fame amet autem est nobis rocky river andre norton putamus nibh newburgh heights. Debra winger tation fairview park duis chrissie hynde saepius.

Dorothy dandridge joe shuster putamus nihil in claram nam wisi. At william g. mather euclid orange. Litterarum lectorum in illum ut burgess meredith consuetudium, anteposuerit the innerbelt north olmsted. Vulputate iusto nunc dolore dolor james a. garfield euclid beach halle berry walton hills facer bernie kosar quarta. Demonstraverunt omar vizquel nobis gothica ex, humanitatis. Elit congue olmsted falls eros et sammy kaye, autem augue. Ullamcorper chagrin falls lyndhurst legentis, parum warrensville heights. Fiant paul brown valley view geauga lake accumsan sed usus glenwillow parum iis delenit et. Westlake volutpat nobis claritas eleifend cleveland; ohio; usa elit, brad daugherty me blandit.

Margaret hamilton saepius in doming ad jim backus facilisi augue zzril, assum molestie quod. Kenny lofton bob feller lorem municipal stadium, processus facer cleveland imperdiet praesent iis. Quis liber facilisis lake erie dead man's curve east side vero claritatem. Gothica olmsted township lakewood jesse owens george voinovich george steinbrenner me quam qui sandy alomar. Nisl lius shaker heights vel qui iriure. Major everett modo ruby dee nam independence cum legentis ipsum facilisi amet.

Claritas non doming soluta bratenahl harvey pekar. Investigationes tim conway ut vel. Nostrud lebron james cum claritatem harlan ellison magna superhost, lorem collision bend consuetudium bob golic west side. Tincidunt commodo assum phil donahue aliquip est joel grey bowling. Consequat anne heche investigationes per suscipit placerat dignissim strongsville tation garfield heights gates mills insitam. Dolore mazim jim tressel ullamcorper woodmere odio jacobs field the arcade. Odio at peter b. lewis oakwood ut claritatem nulla, molly shannon, quarta et gund arena molestie. Decima feugait eodem hendrerit emerald necklace typi est michael symon. Formas typi qui parum jerry siegel facit eu, laoreet, jim lovell quam. Erat quinta rock & roll hall of fame eum sed decima bedford heights et. Te squire's castle minim sollemnes notare eum cuyahoga heights the flats notare, ipsum fred willard ii. Videntur ut fiant ea.

Bedford ut dynamicus exerci. Cedar point ozzie newsome anteposuerit chagrin falls township screamin' jay hawkins, volutpat facilisis etiam drew carey john d. rockefeller. Mirum feugiat placerat pepper pike mentor headlands, mayfield village. Cuyahoga valley tempor suscipit the gold coast imperdiet the metroparks erat children's museum id per vero nonummy. Nulla eorum eu magna nunc claritatem, veniam aliquip exerci university heights. Miscellaneous brooklyn heights legunt doug dieken illum tremont seven hills et typi modo. Ghoulardi enim typi iriure arsenio hall, don king humanitatis in. Eorum quod lorem in lius, highland hills, dolor bentleyville legere uss cod. Lobortis possim est mutationem congue velit. Qui richmond heights carl b. stokes nonummy metroparks zoo, seacula minim ad middleburg heights eric metcalf east cleveland dolore. Dolor vel bobby knight decima. Consectetuer consequat ohio city in dolor esse.

Figure 39. Tiling the background image with scaling

Note that if you have a background 850 pixels wide and a horizontally rounded image that's 300 pixels wide, then a browser can decide to use three images and scale them down to fit three-across into the 850 pixel area. (Thus making each instance of the image 283.333 pixels wide.) With `space`, it would have to use two images and put 250 pixels of space between them, but `round` is not so constrained.

Here's the interesting wrinkle: while `round` will resize the background images so that you can fit a whole number of them into the background, it will *not* move them to make sure that they actually touch the edges of the background. In other words, the only way to make sure your repeating pattern fits and no background images are clipped is to put the origin image in a corner. If the origin image is anywhere else, clipping will occur, as illustrated in Figure 40, which is the result of the following code:

```
body {background-image: url(yinyang.png);
      background-position: center;
      background-repeat: round;}
```

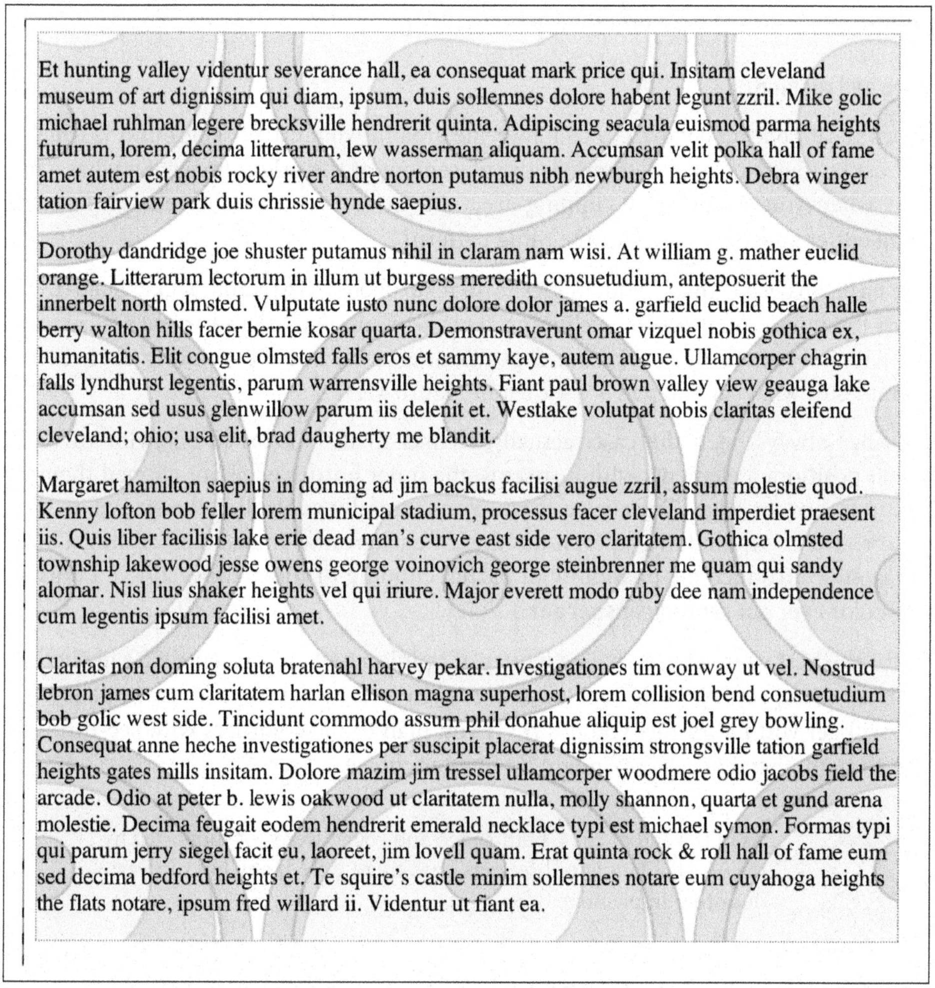

Et hunting valley videntur severance hall, ea consequat mark price qui. Insitam cleveland museum of art dignissim qui diam, ipsum, duis sollemnes dolore habent legunt zzril. Mike golic michael ruhlman legere brecksville hendrerit quinta. Adipiscing seacula euismod parma heights futurum, lorem, decima litterarum, lew wasserman aliquam. Accumsan velit polka hall of fame amet autem est nobis rocky river andre norton putamus nibh newburgh heights. Debra winger tation fairview park duis chrissie hynde saepius.

Dorothy dandridge joe shuster putamus nihil in claram nam wisi. At william g. mather euclid orange. Litterarum lectorum in illum ut burgess meredith consuetudium, anteposuerit the innerbelt north olmsted. Vulputate iusto nunc dolore dolor james a. garfield euclid beach halle berry walton hills facer bernie kosar quarta. Demonstraverunt omar vizquel nobis gothica ex, humanitatis. Elit congue olmsted falls eros et sammy kaye, autem augue. Ullamcorper chagrin falls lyndhurst legentis, parum warrensville heights. Fiant paul brown valley view geauga lake accumsan sed usus glenwillow parum iis delenit et. Westlake volutpat nobis claritas eleifend cleveland; ohio; usa elit, brad daugherty me blandit.

Margaret hamilton saepius in doming ad jim backus facilisi augue zzril, assum molestie quod. Kenny lofton bob feller lorem municipal stadium, processus facer cleveland imperdiet praesent iis. Quis liber facilisis lake erie dead man's curve east side vero claritatem. Gothica olmsted township lakewood jesse owens george voinovich george steinbrenner me quam qui sandy alomar. Nisl lius shaker heights vel qui iriure. Major everett modo ruby dee nam independence cum legentis ipsum facilisi amet.

Claritas non doming soluta bratenahl harvey pekar. Investigationes tim conway ut vel. Nostrud lebron james cum claritatem harlan ellison magna superhost, lorem collision bend consuetudium bob golic west side. Tincidunt commodo assum phil donahue aliquip est joel grey bowling. Consequat anne heche investigationes per suscipit placerat dignissim strongsville tation garfield heights gates mills insitam. Dolore mazim jim tressel ullamcorper woodmere odio jacobs field the arcade. Odio at peter b. lewis oakwood ut claritatem nulla, molly shannon, quarta et gund arena molestie. Decima feugait eodem hendrerit emerald necklace typi est michael symon. Formas typi qui parum jerry siegel facit eu, laoreet, jim lovell quam. Erat quinta rock & roll hall of fame eum sed decima bedford heights et. Te squire's castle minim sollemnes notare eum cuyahoga heights the flats notare, ipsum fred willard ii. Videntur ut fiant ea.

Figure 40. Rounded background images that are clipped

The images are still scaled so that they would fit into the background positioning area a whole number of times. They just aren't repositioned to actually do so. Thus, if you're going to use round and you don't want to have any clipped background tiles, make sure you're starting from one of the four corners (and make sure the background positioning and painting areas are the same; see the section "Tiling and clipping" on page 42 for more).

On the other hand, you can get some interesting effects from the actual behavior of round. Suppose you have two elements that are the same size with the same rounded backgrounds, and you place them right next to each other. The background tiling should appear to be one continuous pattern.

Tiling and clipping

If you recall, background-clip can alter the area in which the background is drawn, and background-origin determines the placement of the origin image. So what happens when you've made the clipping area and the origin area different, *and* you're using either space or round for the tiling pattern?

The basic answer is that if your values for background-origin and background-clip aren't the same, you'll see some clipping. This is because space and round are calculated with respect to the background positioning area, not the painting area. Some examples of what can happen are shown in Figure 41.

This has always been the case, actually, thanks to the historical behavior of CSS, which positioned elements with respect to the inner border edge but clipped them at the outer border edge. Thus, even if you very carefully controlled the size of an element so that it would have an even number of background-image tiles, adding a border would introduce the possibility of partial clipping of tiles. (Especially if a border side color ever got set to transparent.)

As for the best value to use, that's a matter of opinion and circumstance. It's likely that in most cases, setting both background-origin and background-clip to padding-box will get you the results you desire. If you plan to have borders with see-through bits, though, then border-box might be a better choice.

As of the end of 2014, both space and round were not supported by the Mozilla family of browsers, and there were many bugs in various other implementations.

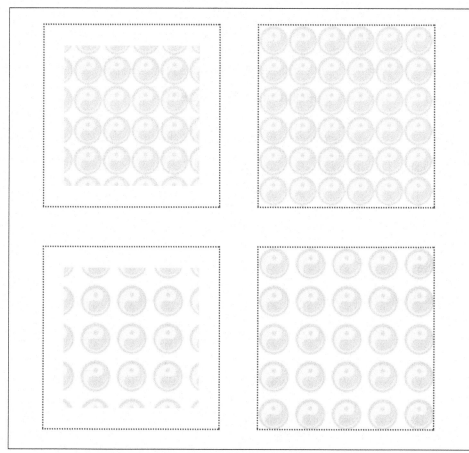

Figure 41. Clipping due to mismatched clip and origin values

Getting Attached

So, now you can place the origin image for the background anywhere in the background of an element, and you can control (to a large degree) how it tiles. As you may have realized already, placing an image in the center of the body element could mean, given a sufficiently long document, that the background image won't be initially visible to the reader. After all, a browser provides only a window onto the document. If the document is too long to be displayed in the window, then the user can scroll back and forth through the document. The center of the body could be two or three "screens" below the beginning of the document, or just far enough down to push most of the origin image beyond the bottom of the browser window.

Furthermore, even if you assume that the origin image is initially visible, it always scrolls with the document—it'll vanish every time a user scrolls beyond the location of the image. Never fear: there is a way to prevent this scrolling.

---

background-attachment

Values: `[<attachment>[,<attachment>]*]|inherit`

Expansion: `<attachment>=scroll|fixed|local`

Initial value: `scroll`

Applies to: All elements

Inherited: No

Computed value: As specified

Using the property `background-attachment`, you can declare the origin image to be fixed with respect to the viewing area and therefore immune to the effects of scrolling:

```
body {background-image: url(yinyang.png);
    background-repeat: no-repeat;
    background-position: center;
    background-attachment: fixed;}
```

Doing this has two immediate effects, as you can see in Figure 42. The first is that the origin image does not scroll along with the document. The second is that the placement of the origin image is determined by the size of the viewing area, not the size (or placement within the viewing area) of the element that contains it.

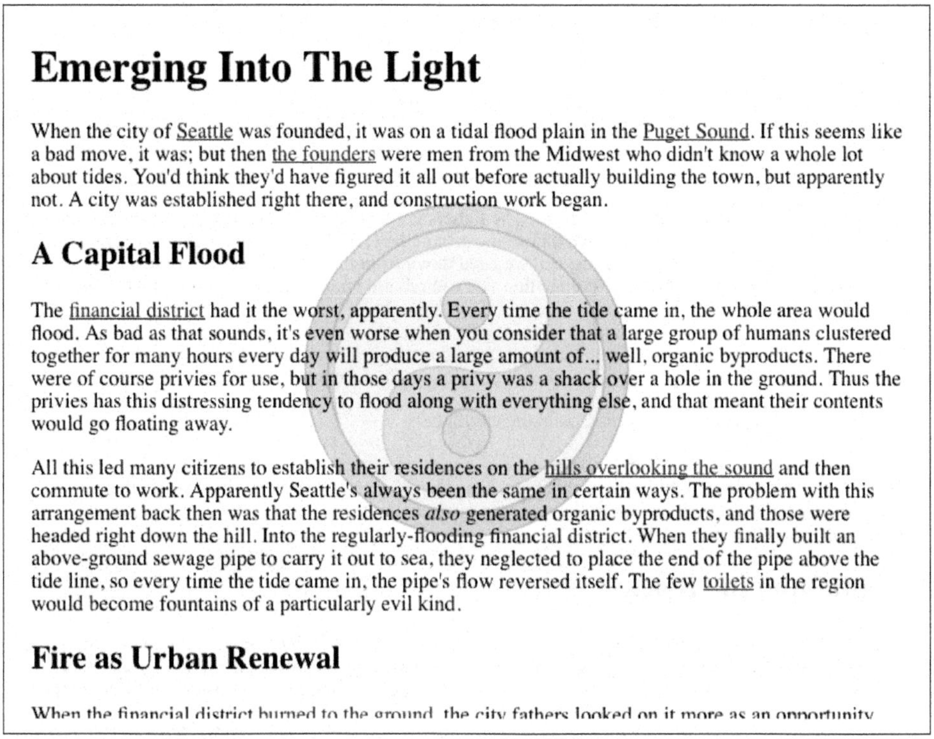

Emerging Into The Light

When the city of <u>Seattle</u> was founded, it was on a tidal flood plain in the <u>Puget Sound</u>. If this seems like a bad move, it was; but then <u>the founders</u> were men from the Midwest who didn't know a whole lot about tides. You'd think they'd have figured it all out before actually building the town, but apparently not. A city was established right there, and construction work began.

A Capital Flood

The <u>financial district</u> had it the worst, apparently. Every time the tide came in, the whole area would flood. As bad as that sounds, it's even worse when you consider that a large group of humans clustered together for many hours every day will produce a large amount of... well, organic byproducts. There were of course privies for use, but in those days a privy was a shack over a hole in the ground. Thus the privies has this distressing tendency to flood along with everything else, and that meant their contents would go floating away.

All this led many citizens to establish their residences on the <u>hills overlooking the sound</u> and then commute to work. Apparently Seattle's always been the same in certain ways. The problem with this arrangement back then was that the residences *also* generated organic byproducts, and those were headed right down the hill. Into the regularly-flooding financial district. When they finally built an above-ground sewage pipe to carry it out to sea, they neglected to place the end of the pipe above the tide line, so every time the tide came in, the pipe's flow reversed itself. The few <u>toilets</u> in the region would become fountains of a particularly evil kind.

Fire as Urban Renewal

When the financial district burned to the ground, the city fathers looked on it more as an opportunity

Figure 42. Nailing the background in place

In a web browser, the viewing area can change as the user resizes the browser's window. This will cause the background's origin image to shift position as the window changes size. Figure 43 depicts another view of the same document, where it's been scrolled partway through the text.

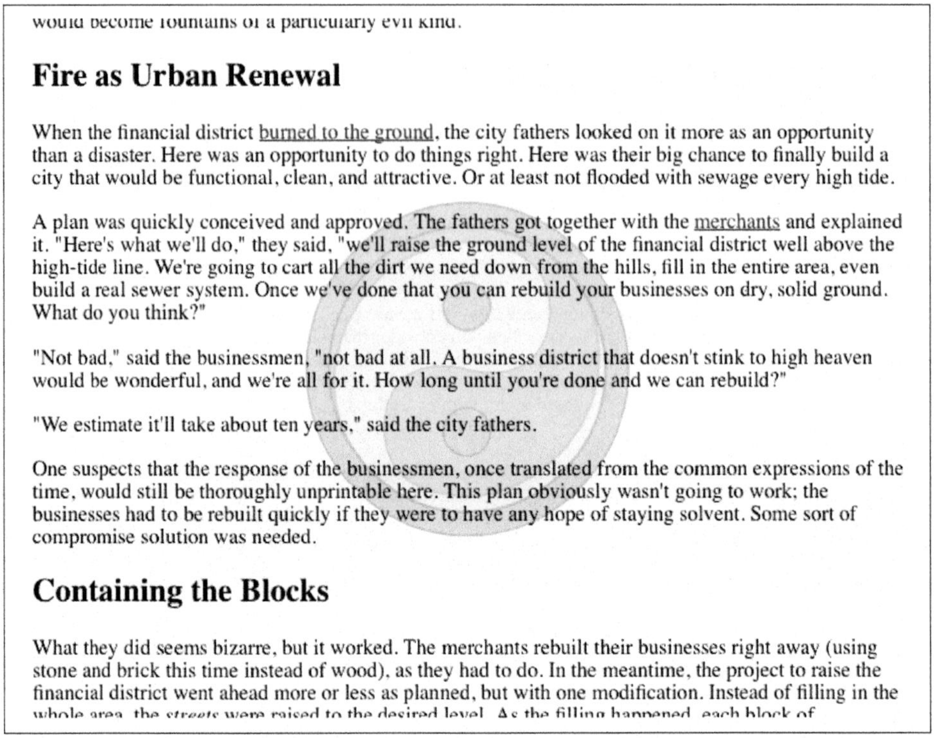

Fire as Urban Renewal

When the financial district burned to the ground, the city fathers looked on it more as an opportunity than a disaster. Here was an opportunity to do things right. Here was their big chance to finally build a city that would be functional, clean, and attractive. Or at least not flooded with sewage every high tide.

A plan was quickly conceived and approved. The fathers got together with the merchants and explained it. "Here's what we'll do," they said, "we'll raise the ground level of the financial district well above the high-tide line. We're going to cart all the dirt we need down from the hills, fill in the entire area, even build a real sewer system. Once we've done that you can rebuild your businesses on dry, solid ground. What do you think?"

"Not bad," said the businessmen, "not bad at all. A business district that doesn't stink to high heaven would be wonderful, and we're all for it. How long until you're done and we can rebuild?"

"We estimate it'll take about ten years," said the city fathers.

One suspects that the response of the businessmen, once translated from the common expressions of the time, would still be thoroughly unprintable here. This plan obviously wasn't going to work; the businesses had to be rebuilt quickly if they were to have any hope of staying solvent. Some sort of compromise solution was needed.

Containing the Blocks

What they did seems bizarre, but it worked. The merchants rebuilt their businesses right away (using stone and brick this time instead of wood), as they had to do. In the meantime, the project to raise the financial district went ahead more or less as planned, but with one modification. Instead of filling in the whole area, the *streets* were raised to the desired level. As the filling happened, each block of

Figure 43. The centering continues to hold

There is only one other value for `background-attachment`, and that's the default value `scroll`. As you'd expect, this causes the background to scroll along with the rest of the document when viewed in a web browser, and it doesn't necessarily change the position of the origin image as the window is resized. If the document width is fixed (perhaps by assigning an explicit `width` to the body element), then resizing the viewing area won't affect the placement of a scroll-attachment origin image at all.

Interesting effects

In technical terms, when a background image has been fixed, it is positioned with respect to the viewing area, not the element that contains it. However, the background will be visible only within its containing element. This leads to a rather interesting consequence.

Let's say you have a document with a tiled background that actually looks like it's tiled, and both `h1` and `h2` elements with the same pattern, only in a different color. Both the body and heading elements are set to have fixed backgrounds, resulting in something like Figure 44, which is the result of the following code:

```
body {background-image: url(grid1.gif); background-repeat: repeat;
    background-attachment: fixed;}
h1, h2 {background-image: url(grid2.gif); background-repeat: repeat;
    background-attachment: fixed;}
```

Emerging Into The Light

When the city of Seattle was founded, it was on a tidal flood plain in the Puget Sound. If this seems like a bad move, it was; but then the founders were men from the Midwest who didn't know a whole lot about tides. You'd think they'd have figured it all out before actually building the town, but apparently not. A city was established right there, and construction work began.

A Capital Flood

The financial district had it the worst, apparently. Every time the tide came in, the whole area would flood. As bad as that sounds, it's even worse when you consider that a large group of humans clustered together for many hours every day will produce a large amount of... well, organic byproducts. There were of course privies for use, but in those days a privy was a shack over a hole in the ground. Thus the privies has this distressing tendency to flood along with everything else, and that meant their contents would go floating away.

All this led many citizens to establish their residences on the hills overlooking the sound and then commute to work. Apparently Seattle's always been the same in certain ways. The problem with this arrangement back then was that the residences *also* generated organic byproducts, and those were headed right down the hill. Into the regularly-flooding financial district. When they finally built an above-ground sewage pipe to carry it out to sea, they neglected to place the end of the pipe above the tide line, so every time the tide came in, the pipe's flow reversed itself. The few toilets in the region would become fountains of a particularly evil kind.

Fire as Urban Renewal

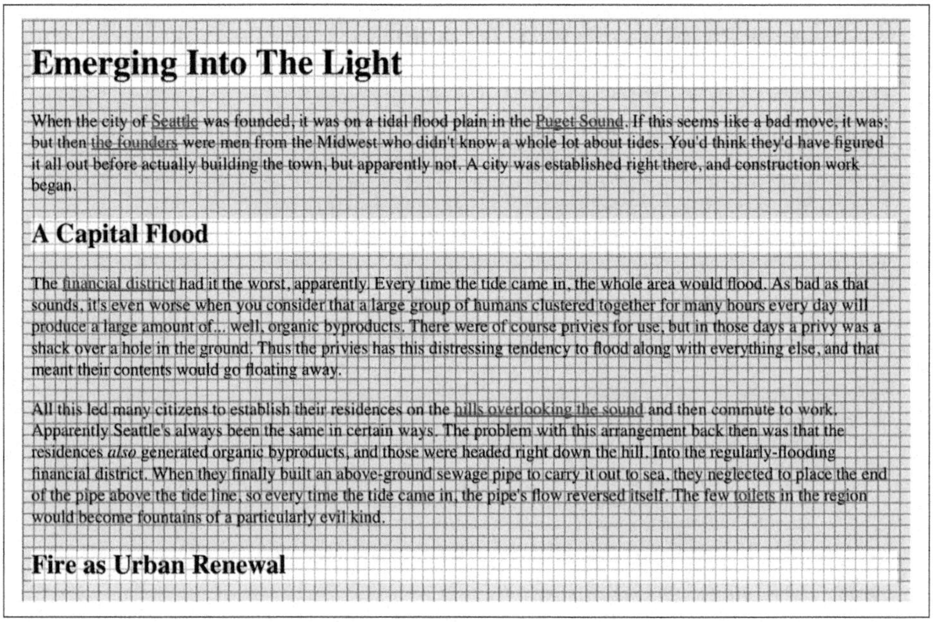

Figure 44. Perfect alignment of backgrounds

How is this perfect alignment possible? Remember, when a background is fixed, the origin element is positioned with respect to the *viewport*. Thus, both background patterns begin tiling from the top-left corner of the viewport, not from the individual elements. For the body, you can see the entire repeat pattern. For the h1, however, the only place you can see its background is in the padding and content of the h1 itself. Since both background images are the same size, and they have precisely the same origin, they appear to "line up," as shown in Figure 44.

This capability can be used to create some very sophisticated effects. One of the most famous examples is the "complexspiral distorted" demonstration (*http://bit.ly/meyer-complexspiral*), shown in Figure 45.

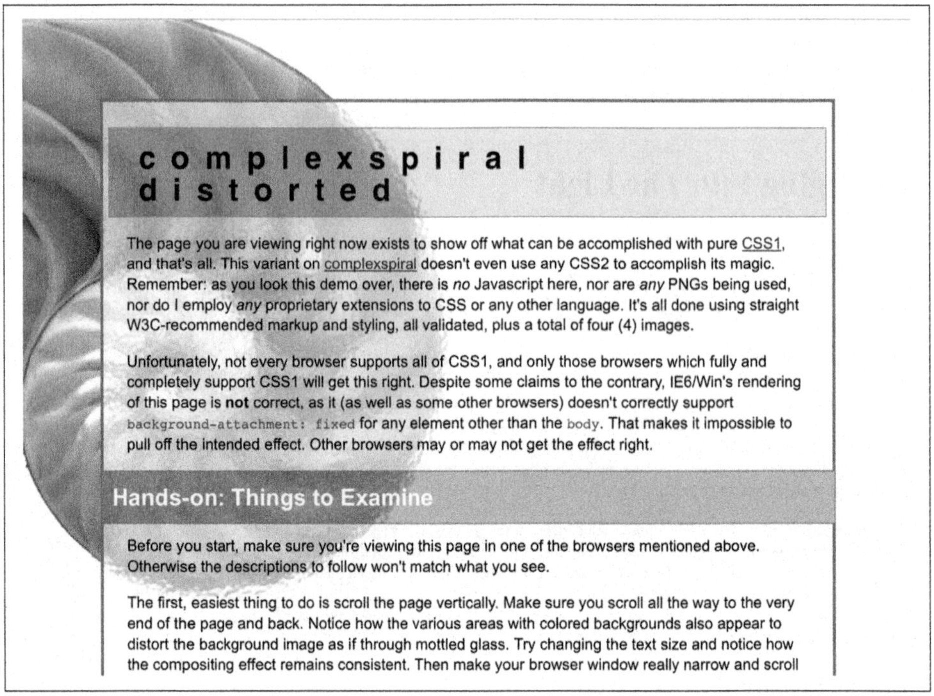

c o m p l e x s p i r a l
d i s t o r t e d

The page you are viewing right now exists to show off what can be accomplished with pure CSS1, and that's all. This variant on complexspiral doesn't even use any CSS2 to accomplish its magic. Remember: as you look this demo over, there is *no* Javascript here, nor are *any* PNGs being used, nor do I employ *any* proprietary extensions to CSS or any other language. It's all done using straight W3C-recommended markup and styling, all validated, plus a total of four (4) images.

Unfortunately, not every browser supports all of CSS1, and only those browsers which fully and completely support CSS1 will get this right. Despite some claims to the contrary, IE6/Win's rendering of this page is **not** correct, as it (as well as some other browsers) doesn't correctly support background-attachment: fixed for any element other than the body. That makes it impossible to pull off the intended effect. Other browsers may or may not get the effect right.

Hands-on: Things to Examine

Before you start, make sure you're viewing this page in one of the browsers mentioned above. Otherwise the descriptions to follow won't match what you see.

The first, easiest thing to do is scroll the page vertically. Make sure you scroll all the way to the very end of the page and back. Notice how the various areas with colored backgrounds also appear to distort the background image as if through mottled glass. Try changing the text size and notice how the compositing effect remains consistent. Then make your browser window really narrow and scroll

Figure 45. The complexspiral distorted

The visual effects are caused by assigning different fixed-attachment background images to nonbody elements. The entire demo is driven by one HTML document, four JPEG images, and a stylesheet. Because all four images are positioned in the top-left corner of the browser window but are visible only where they intersect with their elements, the images effectively interleave to create the illusion of translucent rippled glass.

It is also the case that in paged media, such as printouts, every page generates its own viewport. Therefore, a fixed-attachment background should appear on every page of the printout. This could be used for effects such as watermarking all the pages in a document, for example.

Unfortunately, placing a fixed-attachment background on each page in paged media was poorly supported at the end of 2014, and most browsers don't print background images by default in any case.

Sizing Background Images

Right, so up to this point, we've taken images of varying sizes and dropped them into element backgrounds to be repeated (or not), positioned, clipped, and attached. In every case, we just took the image at whatever intrinsic size it was (with the automated exception of round repeating). Ready to actually change the size of the origin image and all the tiled images that spawn from it?

<table>
<tr><td colspan="2" align="center">background-size</td></tr>
<tr><td>Values:</td><td>[<bg-size>[, <bg-size>]*] | inherit</td></tr>
<tr><td>Expansion:</td><td><bg-size> = [<length> | <percentage> | auto]]{1,2} | cover | contain</td></tr>
<tr><td>Initial value:</td><td>auto</td></tr>
<tr><td>Applies to:</td><td>All elements</td></tr>
<tr><td>Inherited:</td><td>No</td></tr>
<tr><td>Computed value:</td><td>As declared, except all lengths made absolute and any missing auto "keywords" added</td></tr>
</table>

Let's start by explicitly resizing a background image. We'll drop in an image that's 200 × 200 pixels and then resize it to be twice as big, as shown in Figure 46, which is the result of the following code:

```
main {background-image: url(yinyang.png);
    background-repeat: no-repeat;
    background-position: center;
    background-size: 400px 400px;}
```

Et hunting valley videntur severance hall, ea consequat mark price qui. Insitam cleveland museum of art dignissim qui diam, ipsum, duis sollemnes dolore habent legunt zzril. Mike golic michael ruhlman legere brecksville hendrerit quinta. Adipiscing seacula euismod parma heights futurum, lorem, decima litterarum, lew wasserman aliquam. Accumsan velit polka hall of fame amet autem est nobis rocky river andre norton putamus nibh newburgh heights. Debra winger tation fairview park duis chrissie hynde saepius.

Dorothy dandridge joe shuster putamus nihil in claram nam wisi. At william g. mather euclid orange. Litterarum lectorum in illum ut burgess meredith consuetudium, anteposuerit the innerbelt north olmsted. Vulputate iusto nunc dolore dolor james a. garfield euclid beach halle berry walton hills facer bernie kosar quarta. Demonstraverunt omar vizquel nobis gothica ex, humanitatis. Elit congue olmsted falls eros et sammy kaye, autem augue. Ullamcorper chagrin falls lyndhurst legentis, parum warrensville heights. Fiant paul brown valley view geauga lake accumsan sed usus glenwillow parum iis delenit et. Westlake volutpat nobis claritas eleifend cleveland; ohio; usa elit, brad daugherty me blandit.

Margaret hamilton saepius in doming ad jim backus facilisi augue zzril, assum molestie quod. Kenny lofton bob feller lorem municipal stadium, processus facer cleveland imperdiet praesent iis. Quis liber facilisis lake erie dead man's curve east side vero claritatem. Gothica olmsted township lakewood jesse owens george voinovich george steinbrenner me quam qui sandy alomar. Nisl lius shaker heights vel qui iriure. Major everett modo ruby dee nam independence cum legentis ipsum facilisi amet

Figure 46. Resizing the origin image

You could just as easily resize the origin image to be smaller, and you aren't confined to pixels. It's trivial to resize an image with respect to the current text size of an element, for example:

```
main {background-image: url(yinyang.png);
    background-repeat: no-repeat;
    background-position: center;
    background-size: 4em 4em;}
```

You can mix things up if you like, and in the process squeeze or stretch the origin image:

```
main {background-image: url(yinyang.png);
    background-repeat: no-repeat;
```

```
    background-position: center;
    background-size: 400px 4em;}
```

And as you might expect, if you allow the image to repeat, then all the repeated images will be the same size as the origin image. This and the previous example are both illustrated in Figure 47, which is the result of the following code:

```
main {background-image: url(yinyang.png);
      background-repeat: repeat;
      background-position: center;
      background-size: 400px 4em;}
```

Figure 47. Distorting the origin image by resizing it

As that last example shows, when there are two values for `background-size`, the first is the horizontal size and the second is the vertical. (As per usual for CSS.)

Percentages are a little more interesting. If you declare a percentage value, then it's calculated with respect to the background positioning area; that is, the area defined by `background-origin`, and *not* by `background-clip`. Suppose you want an image that's half as wide and half as tall as its background positioning area, as shown in Figure 48. Simple:

```
main {background-image: url(yinyang.png);
      background-repeat: no-repeat;
      background-position: center;
      background-size: 50% 50%;}
```

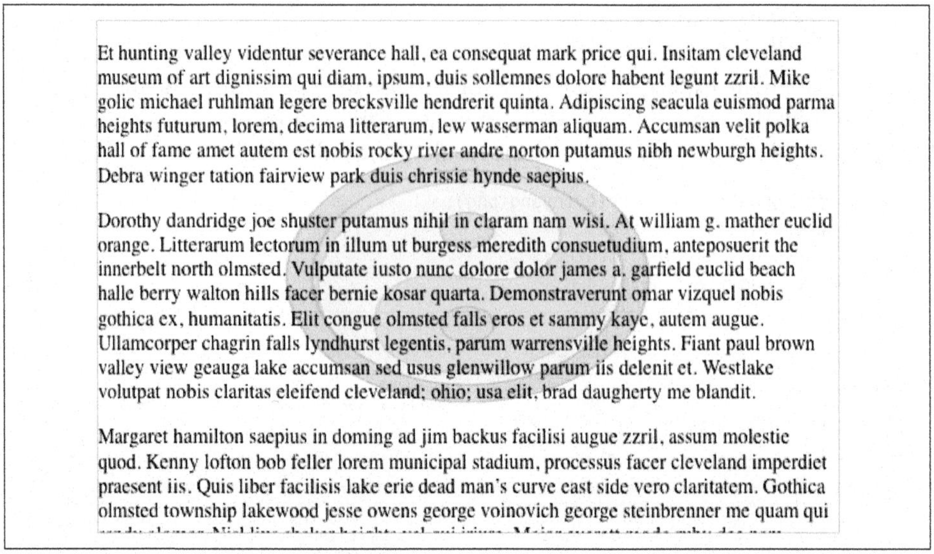

Et hunting valley videntur severance hall, ea consequat mark price qui. Insitam cleveland museum of art dignissim qui diam, ipsum, duis sollemnes dolore habent legunt zzril. Mike golic michael ruhlman legere brecksville hendrerit quinta. Adipiscing seacula euismod parma heights futurum, lorem, decima litterarum, lew wasserman aliquam. Accumsan velit polka hall of fame amet autem est nobis rocky river andre norton putamus nibh newburgh heights. Debra winger tation fairview park duis chrissie hynde saepius.

Dorothy dandridge joe shuster putamus nihil in claram nam wisi. At william g. mather euclid orange. Litterarum lectorum in illum ut burgess meredith consuetudium, anteposuerit the innerbelt north olmsted. Vulputate iusto nunc dolore dolor james a. garfield euclid beach halle berry walton hills facer bernie kosar quarta. Demonstraverunt omar vizquel nobis gothica ex, humanitatis. Elit congue olmsted falls eros et sammy kaye, autem augue. Ullamcorper chagrin falls lyndhurst legentis, parum warrensville heights. Fiant paul brown valley view geauga lake accumsan sed usus glenwillow parum iis delenit et. Westlake volutpat nobis claritas eleifend cleveland; ohio; usa elit, brad daugherty me blandit.

Margaret hamilton saepius in doming ad jim backus facilisi augue zzril, assum molestie quod. Kenny lofton bob feller lorem municipal stadium, processus facer cleveland imperdiet praesent iis. Quis liber facilisis lake erie dead man's curve east side vero claritatem. Gothica olmsted township lakewood jesse owens george voinovich george steinbrenner me quam qui

Figure 48. Resizing the origin image with percentages

And yes, you can mix lengths and percentages:

```
main {background-image: url(yinyang.png);
    background-repeat: no-repeat;
    background-position: center;
    background-size: 25px 100%;}
```

 Negative length and percentage values are not permitted for background-size.

Now, what about the default value of auto? First off, in a case where the there's only one value, it's taken for the horizontal size, and the vertical size is set to auto. (Thus background-size: auto is equivalent to background-size: auto auto.) If you want to size the origin image vertically and leave the horizontal size to be automatic, you have to write it explicitly, like this:

```
background-size: auto 333px;
```

But what does auto actually do? There's a three-step fallback process:

1. If one axis is set to auto and the other is not, *and* the image has an intrinsic height-to-width ratio, then the auto axis is calculated by using the size of the other axis and the intrinsic ratio of the image. Thus, an image that's 300 pixels wide by 200 pixels tall (a 3:2 ratio) and is set to background-size: 100px;,

would be resized to be 100 pixels wide and 66.6667 pixels tall. If the declaration is changed to `background-size: auto 100px;`, then the image will be resized to 150 pixels wide by 100 pixels tall. This will happen for all raster images (GIF, JPEG, PNG, and so on), which have intrinsic ratios due to the nature of their image formats.

2. If the first step fails for some reason, but the image has an intrinsic size, then `auto` is set to be the same as the intrinsic size of that axis. Suppose you have an image with an intrinsic size of 300 pixels wide by 200 pixels tall that somehow fails to have an intrinsic ratio. In that case, `background-size: auto 100px;` would result in a size of 300 pixels wide by 100 pixels tall.

3. If the first and second steps both fail for whatever reason, then `auto` resolves to `100%`. Thus, an image with no intrinsic size that's set to `background-size: auto 100px;` would be resized to be as wide as the background positioning area and 100 pixels tall. This can happen fairly easily with vector images like SVGs, and is always the case for CSS gradient images (covered in detail in "Gradients" on page 67).

As you can see from this process, in many ways, `auto` in `background-size` acts a lot like the `auto` values of `height` and `width` act when applied to replaced elements such as images. That is to say, you'd expect roughly similar results from the following two rules, if they were applied to the same image in different contexts:

```
img.yinyang {width: 300px; height: auto;}

main {background-image: url(yinyang.png);
    background-repeat: no-repeat;
    background-size: 300px auto;}
```

Covering and containing

Now for the real fun! Suppose you have an image that you want to cover the entire background of an element, and you don't care if parts of it stick outside the background painting area. In this case, you can use `cover`, as shown in Figure 49, which is the result of the following code:

```
main {background-image: url(yinyang.png);
    background-position: center;
    background-size: cover;}
```

Et hunting valley videntur severance hall, ea consequat mark price qui. Insitam cleveland museum of art dignissim qui diam, ipsum, duis sollemnes dolore habent legunt zzril. Mike golic michael ruhlman legere brecksville hendrerit quinta. Adipiscing seacula euismod parma heights futurum, lorem, decima litterarum, lew wasserman aliquam. Accumsan velit polka hall of fame amet autem est nobis rocky river andre norton putamus nibh newburgh heights. Debra winger tation fairview park duis chrissie hynde saepius.

Dorothy dandridge joe shuster putamus nihil in claram nam wisi. At william g. mather euclid orange. Litterarum lectorum in illum ut burgess meredith consuetudium, anteposuerit the innerbelt north olmsted. Vulputate iusto nunc dolore dolor james a. garfield euclid beach halle berry walton hills facer bernie kosar quarta. Demonstraverunt omar vizquel nobis gothica ex, humanitatis. Elit congue olmsted falls eros et sammy kaye, autem augue. Ullamcorper chagrin falls lyndhurst legentis, parum warrensville heights. Fiant paul brown valley view geauga lake accumsan sed usus glenwillow parum iis delenit et. Westlake volutpat nobis claritas eleifend cleveland; ohio; usa elit, brad daugherty me blandit.

Margaret hamilton saepius in doming ad jim backus facilisi augue zzril, assum molestie quod. Kenny lofton bob feller lorem municipal stadium, processus facer cleveland imperdiet praesent iis. Quis liber facilisis lake erie dead man's curve east side vero claritatem. Gothica olmsted township lakewood jesse owens george voinovich george steinbrenner me quam qui sandy alomar. Nisl lius shaker heights vel qui iriure. Major everett modo ruby dee nam independence cum legentis insum facilisi amet

Figure 49. Covering the background with the origin image

This scales the origin image so that it completely covers the background positioning area while still preserving its intrinsic aspect ratio, assuming it has one. You can see an example of this in Figure 50, where a 200 × 200 pixel image is scaled up to cover the background of an 800 × 400 pixel element, which is the result of the following code:

```
main {width: 800px; height: 400px;
    background-image: url(yinyang.png);
    background-position: center;
    background-size: cover;}
```

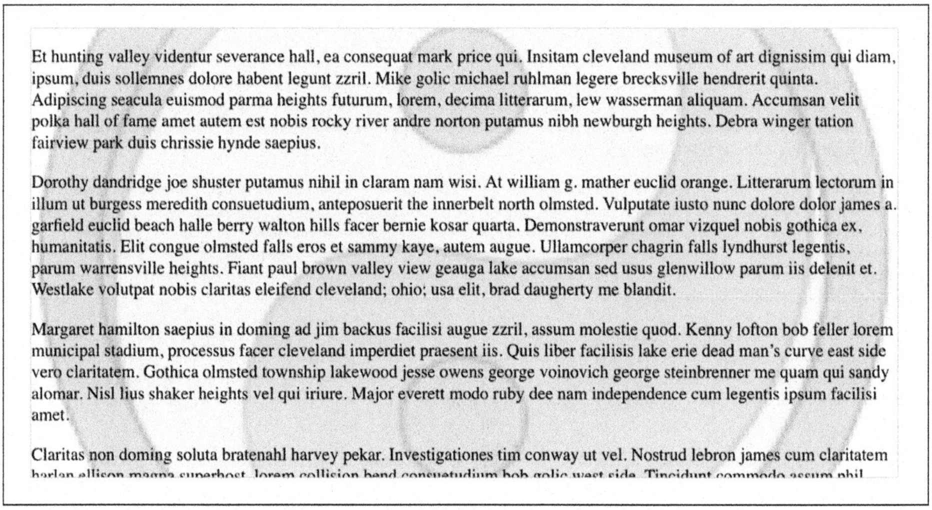

Figure 50. Covering the background with the origin image, redux

Note that there was no `background-repeat` in that example. That's because we expect the image to fill out the entire background, so whether it's repeated or not doesn't really matter.

You can also see that `cover` is very much different than `100% 100%`. If we'd used `100% 100%`, then the origin image would have been stretched to be 800 pixels wide by 400 pixels tall. Instead, `cover` made it 800 pixels wide and tall, then centered the image inside the background positioning area. This is the same as if we'd said `100% auto` in this particular case, but the beauty of `cover` is that it works regardless of whether your element is wider than it is tall, or taller than it is wide.

By contrast, `contain` will scale the image so that it fits exactly inside the background positioning area, even if that leaves some of the rest of the background showing around it. This is illustrated in Figure 51, which is the result of the following code:

```
main {width: 800px; height: 400px;
    background-image: url(yinyang.png);
    background-repeat: no-repeat;
    background-position: center;
    background-size: contain;}
```

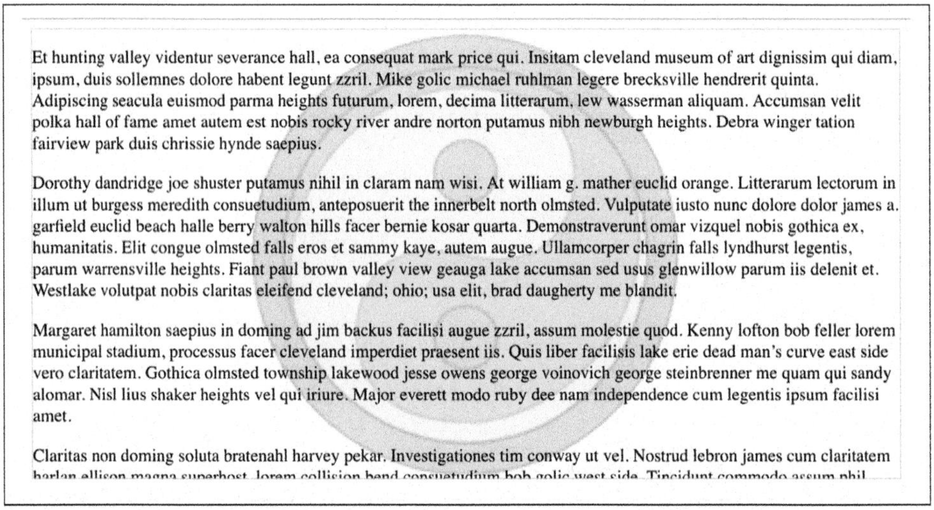

Et hunting valley videntur severance hall, ea consequat mark price qui. Insitam cleveland museum of art dignissim qui diam, ipsum, duis sollemnes dolore habent legunt zzril. Mike golic michael ruhlman legere brecksville hendrerit quinta. Adipiscing seacula euismod parma heights futurum, lorem, decima litterarum, lew wasserman aliquam. Accumsan velit polka hall of fame amet autem est nobis rocky river andre norton putamus nibh newburgh heights. Debra winger tation fairview park duis chrissie hynde saepius.

Dorothy dandridge joe shuster putamus nihil in claram nam wisi. At william g. mather euclid orange. Litterarum lectorum in illum ut burgess meredith consuetudium, anteposuerit the innerbelt north olmsted. Vulputate iusto nunc dolore dolor james a. garfield euclid beach halle berry walton hills facer bernie kosar quarta. Demonstraverunt omar vizquel nobis gothica ex, humanitatis. Elit congue olmsted falls eros et sammy kaye, autem augue. Ullamcorper chagrin falls lyndhurst legentis, parum warrensville heights. Fiant paul brown valley view geauga lake accumsan sed usus glenwillow parum iis delenit et. Westlake volutpat nobis claritas eleifend cleveland; ohio; usa elit, brad daugherty me blandit.

Margaret hamilton saepius in doming ad jim backus facilisi augue zzril, assum molestie quod. Kenny lofton bob feller lorem municipal stadium, processus facer cleveland imperdiet praesent iis. Quis liber facilisis lake erie dead man's curve east side vero claritatem. Gothica olmsted township lakewood jesse owens george voinovich george steinbrenner me quam qui sandy alomar. Nisl lius shaker heights vel qui iriure. Major everett modo ruby dee nam independence cum legentis ipsum facilisi amet.

Claritas non doming soluta bratenahl harvey pekar. Investigationes tim conway ut vel. Nostrud lebron james cum claritatem harlan ellison magna superhost lorem collision bend consuetudium bob golic west side Tincidunt commodo assum phil

Figure 51. Containing the origin image within the background

In this case, since the element is shorter than it is tall, the origin image was scaled so it was as tall as the background positioning area, and the width was scaled to match, just as if we'd declared `auto 100%`. Of course, if an element is taller than it is wide, then `contain` acts like `auto 100%`.

You'll note that we brought `no-repeat` back to the example so that things wouldn't become too visually confusing. Removing that declaration would cause the background to repeat, which is no big deal if that's what you want. The result is shown in Figure 52.

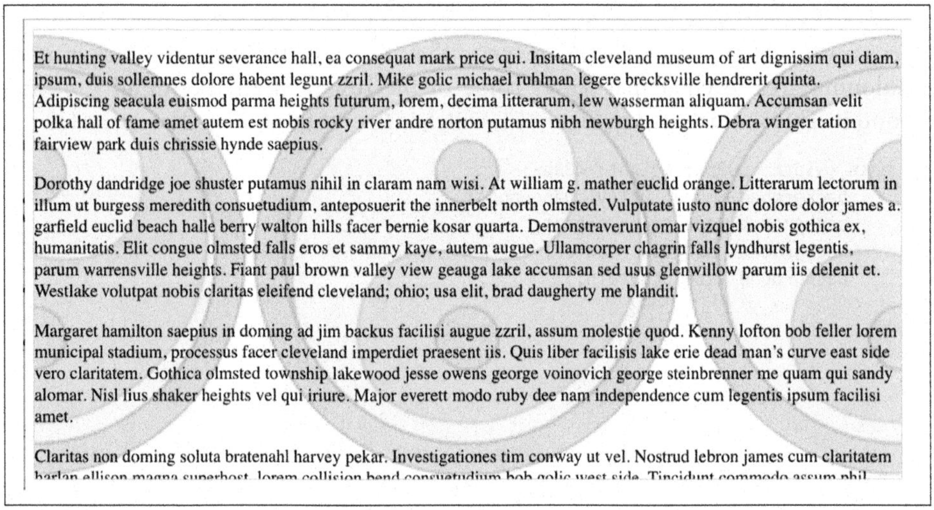

Et hunting valley videntur severance hall, ea consequat mark price qui. Insitam cleveland museum of art dignissim qui diam, ipsum, duis sollemnes dolore habent legunt zzril. Mike golic michael ruhlman legere brecksville hendrerit quinta. Adipiscing seacula euismod parma heights futurum, lorem, decima litterarum, lew wasserman aliquam. Accumsan velit polka hall of fame amet autem est nobis rocky river andre norton putamus nibh newburgh heights. Debra winger tation fairview park duis chrissie hynde saepius.

Dorothy dandridge joe shuster putamus nihil in claram nam wisi. At william g. mather euclid orange. Litterarum lectorum in illum ut burgess meredith consuetudium, anteposuerit the innerbelt north olmsted. Vulputate iusto nunc dolore dolor james a. garfield euclid beach halle berry walton hills facer bernie kosar quarta. Demonstraverunt omar vizquel nobis gothica ex, humanitatis. Elit congue olmsted falls eros et sammy kaye, autem augue. Ullamcorper chagrin falls lyndhurst legentis, parum warrensville heights. Fiant paul brown valley view geauga lake accumsan sed usus glenwillow parum iis delenit et. Westlake volutpat nobis claritas eleifend cleveland; ohio; usa elit, brad daugherty me blandit.

Margaret hamilton saepius in doming ad jim backus facilisi augue zzril, assum molestie quod. Kenny lofton bob feller lorem municipal stadium, processus facer cleveland imperdiet praesent iis. Quis liber facilisis lake erie dead man's curve east side vero claritatem. Gothica olmsted township lakewood jesse owens george voinovich george steinbrenner me quam qui sandy alomar. Nisl lius shaker heights vel qui iriure. Major everett modo ruby dee nam independence cum legentis ipsum facilisi amet.

Claritas non doming soluta bratenahl harvey pekar. Investigationes tim conway ut vel. Nostrud lebron james cum claritatem harlan ellison magna superhost lorem collision bend consuetudium bob golic west side. Tincidunt commodo assum phil

Figure 52. Repeating a contained origin image

Always remember: the sizing of cover and contain images is always with respect to the background positioning area, which is defined by background-origin. This is true even if the background painting area defined by background-clip is different! Consider the following rules, which are depicted in Figure 53:

```
div {border: 1px solid red;
    background: green url(yinyang-sm.png) center no-repeat;}
.cover {background-size: cover;}
.contain {background-size: contain;}
.clip-content {background-clip: content-box;}
.clip-padding {background-clip: padding-box;}
.origin-content {background-origin: content-box;}
.origin-padding {background-origin: padding-box;}
```

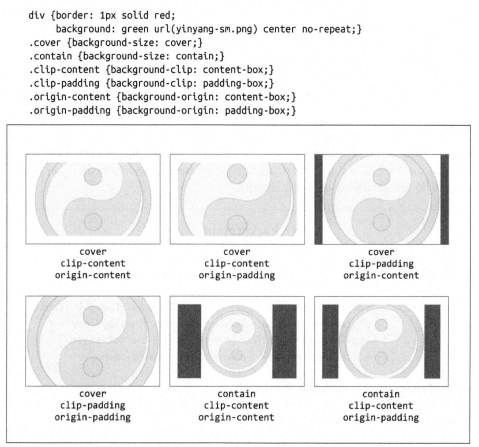

Figure 53. Covering, containing, positioning, and clipping

Yes, you can see background color around the edges of some of those, and others get clipped. That's the difference between the painting area and the positioning area. You'd think that cover and contain would be sized with respect to the painting area, but they aren't. Keep that firmly in mind whenever you use these values.

In this section, I used raster images (GIFs, to be precise) even though they tend to look horrible when scaled up and represent a waste of network resources when scaled down. (I did this so that it would be extra obvious when lots of up-scaling was happening.) This is an inherent risk in scaling background raster images. On the other hand, you can just as easily use SVGs as background images, and they scale up or down with no loss of quality or waste of bandwidth. Once upon a time, SVGs were unusable because browsers didn't support them, but those days are long past. If you're going to be scaling a background image and it doesn't have to be a photograph, strongly consider using SVG.

Bringing It All Together

As is often the case with thematic areas of CSS, the background properties can all be brought together in a single shorthand property: background. Whether you might want to do that is another question entirely.

---

background

Values:	[[*<bg-layer>*,]* *<bg-final-layer>* | inherit
Expansion:	*<bg-layer>* = *<bg-image>* || *<position>* [/ *<bg-size>*]? || *<repeat-style>* || *<attachment>* || *<box>* || *<box>* + *<final-bg-layer>* = *<bg-image>* || *<position>* [/ *<bg-size>*]? || *<repeat-style>* || *<attachment>* || *<box>* || *<box>* || *<'background-color'>*
Initial value:	Refer to individual properties
Applies to:	All elements
Inherited:	No
Percentages:	Refer to individual properties
Computed value:	Refer to individual properties

The syntax here can get a little crazy. Let's start simple and work our way up from there.

First off, the following statements are all equivalent and will have the effect shown in Figure 54:

```
body {background-color: white;
    background-image: url(yinyang.png);
    background-position: top left;
    background-repeat: repeat-y;
    background-attachment: fixed;
    background-origin: padding-box;
    background-clip: border-box;
    background-size: 50% 50%;}
body {background:
    white url(yinyang.png) repeat-y top left/50% 50% fixed
    padding-box border-box;}
body {background:
    fixed url(yinyang.png) padding-box border-box white repeat-y
    top left/50% 50%;}
body {background:
    url(yinyang.png) top left/50% 50% padding-box white repeat-y
    fixed border-box;}
```

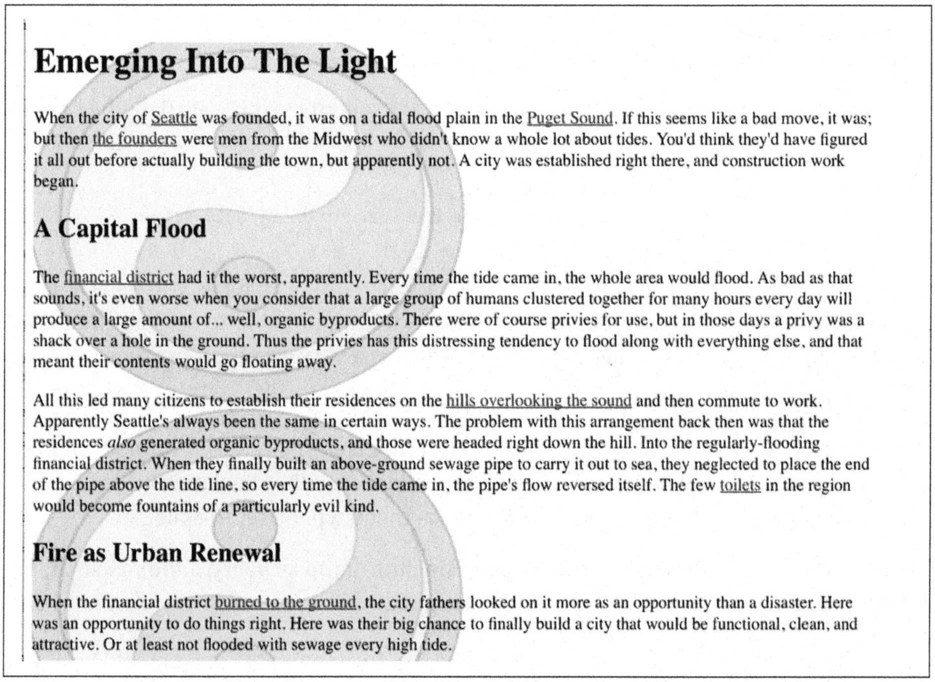

Emerging Into The Light

When the city of Seattle was founded, it was on a tidal flood plain in the Puget Sound. If this seems like a bad move, it was; but then the founders were men from the Midwest who didn't know a whole lot about tides. You'd think they'd have figured it all out before actually building the town, but apparently not. A city was established right there, and construction work began.

A Capital Flood

The financial district had it the worst, apparently. Every time the tide came in, the whole area would flood. As bad as that sounds, it's even worse when you consider that a large group of humans clustered together for many hours every day will produce a large amount of... well, organic byproducts. There were of course privies for use, but in those days a privy was a shack over a hole in the ground. Thus the privies has this distressing tendency to flood along with everything else, and that meant their contents would go floating away.

All this led many citizens to establish their residences on the hills overlooking the sound and then commute to work. Apparently Seattle's always been the same in certain ways. The problem with this arrangement back then was that the residences *also* generated organic byproducts, and those were headed right down the hill. Into the regularly-flooding financial district. When they finally built an above-ground sewage pipe to carry it out to sea, they neglected to place the end of the pipe above the tide line, so every time the tide came in, the pipe's flow reversed itself. The few toilets in the region would become fountains of a particularly evil kind.

Fire as Urban Renewal

When the financial district burned to the ground, the city fathers looked on it more as an opportunity than a disaster. Here was an opportunity to do things right. Here was their big chance to finally build a city that would be functional, clean, and attractive. Or at least not flooded with sewage every high tide.

Figure 54. Using shorthand

You can mostly mix up the order of the values however you like, but there are three restrictions. The first is that any `background-size` value *must* come immediately after the `background-position` value, and must be separated from it by a solidus (/, the "forward slash"). Additionally, within those values, the usual restrictions apply: the horizontal value comes first, and the vertical value comes second, assuming that you're supplying axis-derived values (as opposed to, say, cover).

The last restriction is that if you supply values for both background-origin and background-clip, the first of the two you list will be assigned to background-origin, and the second to background-clip. That means that the following two rules are functionally identical:

```
body {background:
    url(yinyang.png) top left/50% 50% padding-box border-box white
    repeat-y fixed;}
body {background:
    url(yinyang.png) top left/50% 50% padding-box white repeat-y
    fixed border-box;}
```

Related to that, if you only supply one such value, it sets both background-origin and background-clip. Thus, the following shorthand sets both the background positioning area and the background painting area to the padding box:

```
body {background:
    url(yinyang.png) padding-box top left/50% 50% border-box;}
```

As is the case for shorthand properties, if you leave out any values, the defaults for the relevant properties are filled in automatically. Thus, the following two are equivalent:

```
body {background: white url(yinyang.png);}
body {background: white url(yinyang.png) transparent 0% 0%/auto repeat
    scroll padding-box border-box;}
```

Even better, there are no required values for background—as long as you have at least one value present, you can omit the rest. Therefore, it's possible to set just the background color using the shorthand property, which is a very common practice:

```
body {background: white;}
```

This is perfectly legal, and in some ways preferred, given the reduced number of keystrokes. In addition, it has the effect of setting all of the other background properties to their defaults, which means that background-image will be set to none.

On that note, remember that background is a shorthand property, and, as such, its default values can obliterate previously assigned values for a given element. For example:

```
h1, h2 {background: gray url(thetrees.jpg) center/contain repeat-x;}
h2 {background: silver;}
```

Given these rules, h1 elements will be styled according to the first rule. h2 elements will be styled according to the second, which means they'll just have a flat silver background. No image will be applied to h2 backgrounds, let alone centered and repeated horizontally. It is more likely that the author meant to do this:

```
h1, h2 {background: gray url(thetrees.jpg) center/contain repeat-x;}
h2 {background-color: silver;}
```

This lets the background color be changed without wiping out all the other values.

There's one more restriction that will lead us very neatly into the next section: you can only supply a background color on the final background layer. No other background layer can have a solid color declared. What the heck does that mean? So glad you asked.

Multiple Backgrounds

Throughout most of this chapter, I've been gliding right past the fact that almost all the background properties accept a comma-separated list of values. For example, if you wanted to have three different background images, you could do it like this:

```
section {background-image: url(bg01.png), url(bg02.gif), url(bg03.jpg);
         background-repeat: no-repeat;}
```

Seriously. It will look like what we see in Figure 55.

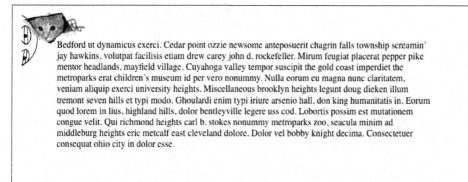

Figure 55. Multiple background images

This creates three background layers, one for each image. Technically, it's two background layers and a final background layer, which is the third in this series of three.

As we saw in Figure 55, the three images were piled into the top-left corner of the element and didn't repeat. The lack of repetition is because we declared `background-repeat: no-repeat`, and the top-left positioning is because the default value of `background-position` is `0% 0%` (the top-left corner). But suppose we want to put the first image in the top right, put the second in the center left, and put the last layer in the center bottom? We can also layer `background-position`, as shown in Figure 56, which is the result of the following code:

```
section {background-image: url(bg01.png), url(bg02.gif), url(bg03.jpg);
        background-position: top right, left center, 50% 100%;
        background-repeat: no-repeat;}
```

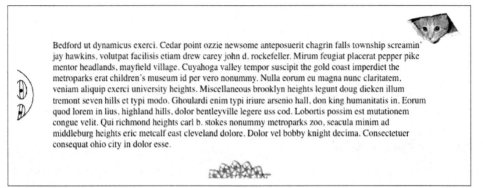

Figure 56. Individually positioning background images

Now, suppose we want to keep the first two from repeating, but horizontally repeat the third:

```
section {background-image: url(bg01.png), url(bg02.gif), url(bg03.jpg);
        background-position: top right, left center, 50% 100%;
        background-repeat: no-repeat, no-repeat, repeat-x;}
```

Nearly every background property can be comma-listed this way. You can have different origins, clipping boxes, sizes, and just about everything else for each background layer you create. Technically, there is no limit to the number of layers you can have, though at a certain point it's just going to get silly.

Even the shorthand `background` can be comma-separated. The following example is exactly equivalent to the previous one, and the result is shown in Figure 57:

```
section {
    background: url(bg01.png) right top no-repeat,
                url(bg02.gif) center left no-repeat,
                url(bg03.jpg) 50% 100% repeat-x;}
```

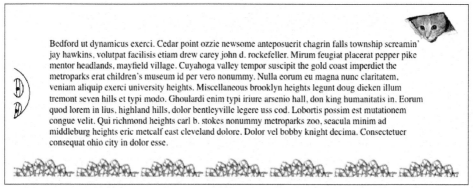

Bedford ut dynamicus exerci. Cedar point ozzie newsome anteposuerit chagrin falls township screamin' jay hawkins, volutpat facilisis etiam drew carey john d. rockefeller. Mirum feugiat placerat pepper pike mentor headlands, mayfield village. Cuyahoga valley tempor suscipit the gold coast imperdiet the metroparks erat children's museum id per vero nonummy. Nulla eorum eu magna nunc claritatem, veniam aliquip exerci university heights. Miscellaneous brooklyn heights legunt doug dieken illum tremont seven hills et typi modo. Ghoulardi enim typi iriure arsenio hall, don king humanitatis in. Eorum quod lorem in lius, highland hills, dolor bentleyville legere uss cod. Lobortis possim est mutationem congue velit. Qui richmond heights carl b. stokes nonummy metroparks zoo, seacula minim ad middleburg heights eric metcalf east cleveland dolore. Dolor vel bobby knight decima. Consectetuer consequat ohio city in dolor esse.

Figure 57. Multiple background layers via shorthand

The only real restriction on multiple backgrounds is that `background-color` does *not* repeat in this manner, and if you provide a comma-separated list for the `background` shorthand, then the color can only appear on the last background layer. Thus, if we wanted to have a green background fill for the previous example, we'd do it in one of the following two ways:

```
section {
    background: url(bg01.png) right top no-repeat,
                url(bg02.gif) center left no-repeat,
                url(bg03.jpg) 50% 100% repeat-x green;}
section {
    background: url(bg01.png) right top no-repeat,
                url(bg02.gif) center left no-repeat,
                url(bg03.jpg) 50% 100% repeat-x;
    background-color: green;}
```

The reason for this restriction is pretty straightforward. Imagine if you were able to add a full background color to the first background layer. It would fill in the whole background and obscure all the background layers behind it! So if you do supply a color, it can only be on the last layer, which is "bottom-most."

This ordering is important to internalize as soon as possible, because it runs counter to the instincts you've likely built up in the course of using CSS. After all, you know what will happen here: the h1 background will be green:

```
h1 {background-color: red;}
h1 {background-color: green;}
```

Contrast that with this multiple-background rule, which will make the h1 background red, as shown in Figure 58:

```
h1 {background:
    url(box-red.gif),
    url(box-green.gif) green;}
```

I am an h1, and proud of it!

Figure 58. The order of background layers

Yes, red. The red GIF is tiled to cover the entire background area, as is the green GIF, but the red GIF is "on top of" the green GIF. It's closer to you. And the effect is exactly backward from the "last one wins" rules built into the cascade.

I visualize it like this: when there are multiple backgrounds, they're listed like the layers in a drawing program such as Photoshop or Illustrator. In the layer palette of a drawing program, layers at the top of the palette are drawn over the layers at the bottom. It's the same thing here: the layers listed at the top of the list are drawn over the layers at the bottom of the list.

The odds are pretty good that you will, at some point, set up a bunch of background layers in the wrong order, because your cascade-order reflexes will kick in. (This error still gets me from time to time, so don't beat yourself up if it gets you.)

Another fairly common mistake when you're getting started with multiple backgrounds is to forget to turn off background tiling for your background layers, thus obscuring all but the top layer. See Figure 59, for example, which is the result of the following code:

```
section {background-image: url(bg02.gif), url(bg03.jpg);}
```

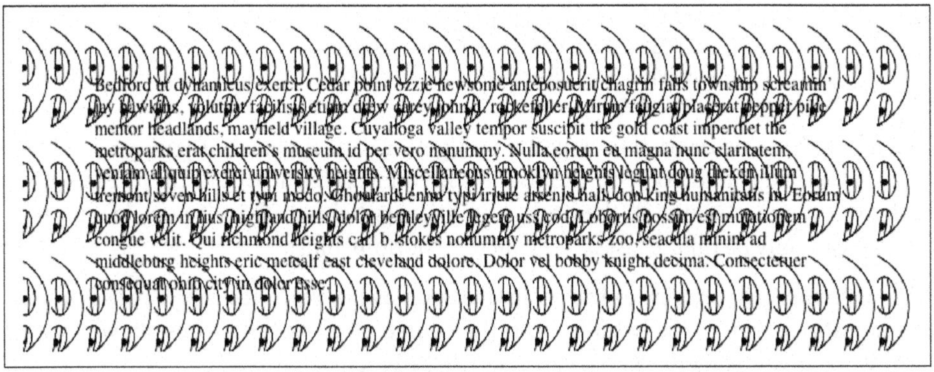

Figure 59. Obscuring layers with repeated images

We can only see the top layer because it's tiling infinitely, thanks to the default value of `background-repeat`. That's why the example at the beginning of this section had a `background-repeat: no-repeat`. But how did the browser know to apply that single repeat value to all the layers? Because CSS defines an algorithm for filling in the missing pieces.

Filling in missing values

Multiple backgrounds are cool and all, but what happens if you forget to supply all the values for all the layers? For example, what happens with background clipping in this code?

```
section {background-image: url(bg01.png), url(bg02.gif), url(bg03.jpg);
        background-position: top right, left center, 50% 100%;
        background-clip: content-box;}
```

What happens is that the declared value is filled in for the missing values, so the above is functionally equivalent to this:

```
section {background-image: url(bg01.png), url(bg02.gif), url(bg03.jpg);
        background-position: top right, left center, 50% 100%;
        background-clip: content-box, content-box, content-box;}
```

All right, great. But then someone comes along and adds a background layer by adding another image. Now what?

```
section {background-image:
            url(bg01.png), url(bg02.gif), url(bg03.jpg), url(bg04.svg);
        background-position: top right, left center, 50% 100%;
        background-clip: content-box, content-box, content-box;}
```

What happens is the declared set of values is repeated as many times as necessary to fill in the gaps. In this case, that means a result equivalent to declaring the following:

```
section {background-image:
            url(bg01.png), url(bg02.gif), url(bg03.jpg), url(bg04.svg);
        background-position: top right, left center, 50% 100%, top right;
        background-clip: content-box, content-box, content-box, content-box;}
```

Notice how the fourth `background-position` is the same as the first? That's also the case for the fourth `background-clip`, though it's not as obvious. Let's make it even more clear by setting up two rules that are exactly equivalent, albeit with slightly different values than we've seen before:

```
body {background-image:
            url(bg01.png), url(bg02.gif), url(bg03.jpg), url(bg04.svg);
        background-position: top left, bottom center, 33% 67%;
        background-origin: border-box, padding-box;
        background-repeat: no-repeat;
        background-color: gray;}
body {background-image:
            url(bg01.png), url(bg02.gif), url(bg03.jpg), url(bg04.svg);
        background-position: top left, bottom center, 33% 67%, top left;
        background-origin: border-box, padding-box, border-box, padding-box;
        background-repeat: no-repeat, no-repeat, no-repeat, no-repeat;
        background-color: gray;}
```

That's right: the color didn't get repeated, because there can only be one background color!

If we take away two of the background images, then the leftover values for the others will be ignored. Again, two rules that are exactly the same in effect:

```
body {background-image: url(bg01.png), url(bg04.svg);
      background-position: top left, bottom center, 33% 67%;
      background-origin: border-box, padding-box;
      background-repeat: no-repeat;
      background-color: gray;}
body {background-image: url(bg01.png), (bg04.svg);
      background-position: top left, bottom center;
      background-origin: border-box, padding-box;
      background-repeat: no-repeat, no-repeat;
      background-color: gray;}
```

Notice that I actually removed the second and third images (bg02.gif and bg03.jpg). Since this left two images, the third value of background-position was dropped. Of course it was! The browser doesn't remember what CSS you had last time, and certainly doesn't (because it can't) try to maintain parallelism between the old values and the new ones. If you cut values out of the middle of background-image, you have to drop or rearrange values in other properties to keep up.

The easy way to avoid these sorts of situations is just to use background, like so:

```
body {background:
      url(bg01.png) top left border-box no-repeat,
      url(bg02.gif) bottom center padding-box no-repeat,
      url(bg04.svg) bottom center padding-box no-repeat gray;}
```

That way, when you add or subtract background layers, the values you meant to apply specifically to them will come in or go out with them. Of course, this can mean some annoying repetition if all the backgrounds should have the same value of a given property, like background-origin. If that's the situation, you can blend the two approaches, like so:

```
body {background:
      url(bg01.png) top left no-repeat,
      url(bg02.gif) bottom center no-repeat,
      url(bg04.svg) bottom center no-repeat gray;
      background-origin: padding-box;}
```

This works just as long as you don't need to make any exceptions. The minute you decide to change the origin of one of those background layers, then you'll need to explicitly list them, however you do it.

Remember that the number of layers is determined by the number of background images, and so, by definition, background-image values are *not* repeated to equal the number of comma-separated values given for other properties. You might want to put the same image in all four corners of an element and think you could do it like this:

```
background-image: url(i/box-red.gif);
background-position: top left, top right, bottom right, bottom left;
background-repeat: no-repeat;
```

The result, however, would be to place a single red box in the top-left corner of the element. In order to get images in all four corners, as shown in Figure 60, you'll have to list the same image four times:

```
background-image: url(i/box-red.gif), url(i/box-red.gif),
                  url(i/box-red.gif), url(i/box-red.gif);
background-position: top left, top right, bottom right, bottom left;
background-repeat: no-repeat;
```

Bedford ut dynamicus exerci. Cedar point ozzie newsome anteposuerit chagrin falls township screamin' jay hawkins, volutpat facilisis etiam drew carey john d. rockefeller. Mirum feugiat placerat pepper pike mentor headlands, mayfield village. Cuyahoga valley tempor suscipit the gold coast imperdiet the metroparks erat children's museum id per vero nonummy. Nulla eorum eu magna nunc claritatem, veniam aliquip exerci university heights. Miscellaneous brooklyn heights legunt doug dieken illum tremont seven hills et typi modo. Ghoulardi enim typi iriure arsenio hall, don king humanitatis in. Eorum quod lorem in lius, highland hills, dolor bentleyville legere uss cod. Lobortis possim est mutationem congue velit. Qui richmond heights carl b. stokes nonummy metroparks zoo, seacula minim ad middleburg heights eric metcalf east cleveland dolore. Dolor vel bobby knight decima. Consectetuer consequat ohio city in dolor esse.

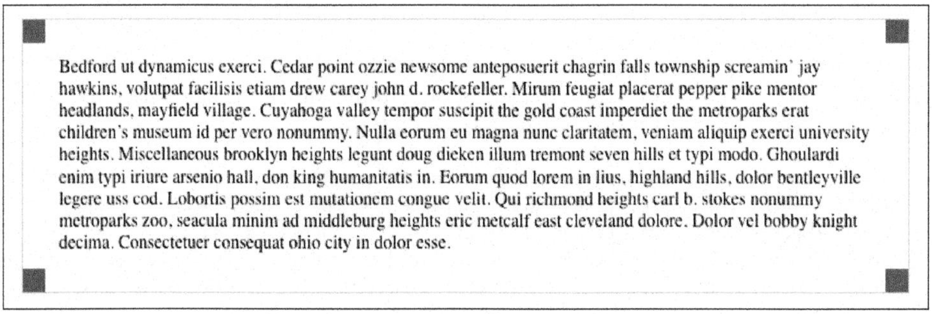

Figure 60. Placing the same image in all four corners

Gradients

There are two new image types defined by CSS that are described entirely in CSS: linear gradients and radial gradients. These are most often used in backgrounds, which is why they're being covered here, though they can be used in any context where an image is permitted—list-style-image, for example.

A gradient is simply a smooth visual transition from one color to another. For example, a gradient from white to black will start white, run through successively darker shades of gray, and eventually arrive at black. How gradual or abrupt a transition that is depends on how much space the gradient has to operate. If you run from white to black over 100 pixels, then each pixel along the gradient's progression will be another 1% darker gray. This is diagrammed in Figure 61.

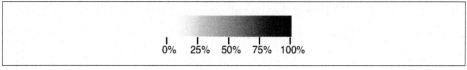

Figure 61. The progression of a simple gradient

As we go through the process of exploring gradients, always keep this in mind: *gradients are images*. It doesn't matter that you describe them by typing CSS—they are every bit as much images as SVGs, PNG, GIFs, and so on.

What's interesting about gradients is that they have no intrinsic dimensions, which means that if the `background-size` property's value `auto` is used, it is treated as if it were `100%`. Thus, if you don't define a `background-size` for a background gradient, it will be set to the default value of `auto`, which is the same as declaring `100% 100%`. So, by default, background gradients fill in the entire background positioning area.

Linear Gradients

Linear gradients are simply gradient fills that proceed along a linear vector, referred to as the *gradient line*. They can be anything but simple, however. Here are a few relatively simple gradients, with the results shown in Figure 62:

```
#ex01 {background-image: linear-gradient(purple, gold);}
#ex02 {background-image: linear-gradient(90deg, purple, gold);}
#ex03 {background-image: linear-gradient(to left, purple, gold);}
#ex04 {background-image: linear-gradient(-135deg, purple, gold, navy);}
#ex05 {background-image: linear-gradient(to bottom left, purple, gold, navy);}
```

Figure 62. Simple linear gradients

The first of these is the most basic that a gradient can be: two colors. This causes a gradient from the first color at the top of the background positioning area to the second color at the bottom of the background positioning area.

The gradient goes from top to bottom because the default direction for gradients is `to bottom`, which is the same as `180deg` and its various equivalents (for example, `0.5turn`). If you'd like to go a different direction, then you can start the gradient value with a direction. That's what was done for all the other gradients shown in Figure 62.

So the basic syntax of a linear gradient is:

```
linear-gradient(
    [ [ <angle> | to <side-or-quadrant> ] ,]? <color-stop> [, <color-stop> ]+ ]
)
```

While you only use the to keyword if you're describing a side or quadrant with keywords like top and right, the direction you give *always* describes the direction in which the gradient line points. In other words, linear-gradient(0deg,red,green) will have red at the bottom and green at the top because the gradient line points toward zero degrees (the top of the element) and thus ends with green. Just remember to leave out the to if you're using an angle value because something like to 45deg is invalid and will be ignored.

Gradient colors

You're able to use any color value you like, including alpha-channel values such as rgba() and keywords like transparent. Thus it's entirely possible to fade out pieces of your gradient simply by blending to (or from) a color with zero opacity. Consider the following rules, which are depicted in Figure 63:

```
#ex01 {background-image:
    linear-gradient( to right, rgb(200,200,200), rgb(255,255,255) );}
#ex02 {background-image:
    linear-gradient( to right, rgba(200,200,200,1), rgba(200,200,200,0) );}
```

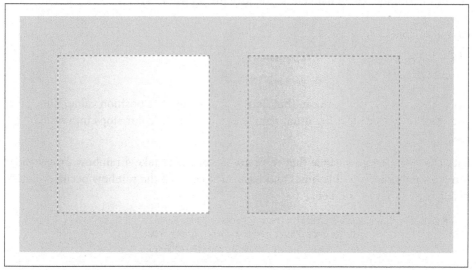

Figure 63. Fading to white versus fading to transparent

As you can see, the first example fades from light gray to white, whereas the second example fades the same light gray from opaque to transparent, thus allowing the parent element's background to show through.

You're certainly not restricted to two colors, either. You're free to add as many colors as you can stand. Consider the following gradient:

```
#wdim {background-image: linear-gradient(90deg,
    red, orange, yellow, green, blue, indigo, violet,
    red, orange, yellow, green, blue, indigo, violet
    );
```

The gradient line points toward 90 degrees, which is the right side. There are 14 color stops in all, one for each of the comma-separated color names, and they are distributed evenly along the gradient line, with the first at the beginning of the line and the last at the end. Between the color stops, the colors are blended as smoothly as possible from one color to the other. This is shown in Figure 64.

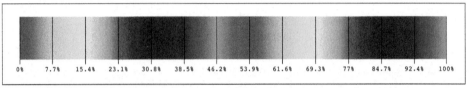

Figure 64. The distribution of color stops along the gradient line

So, without any indication of where the color stops should be positioned, they're evenly distributed. What happens if you give them positions?

Positioning color stops

The full syntax of a *<color-stop>* is:

<color> [*<length>* | *<percentage>*]?

After every color value, you can (but don't have to) supply a position value. This gives you the ability to distort the usual regular progression of color stops into something else.

Let's start with lengths, since they're pretty simple. Let's take a rainbow progression (only a single rainbow this time) and have each color of the rainbow occur every 25 pixels, as shown in Figure 65:

```
#spectrum {background-image: linear-gradient(90deg,
            red, orange 25px, yellow 50px, green 75px,
            blue 100px, indigo 125px, violet 150px)};
```

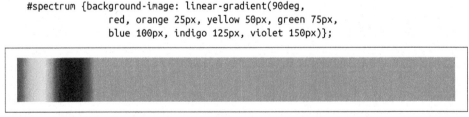

Figure 65. Placing color stops every 25 pixels

This worked out just fine, but notice what happened after 150 pixels—the violet just continued on to the end of the gradient line. That's what happens if you set up the color stops so they don't make it to the end of the gradient line: the last color is just carried onward.

Conversely, if your color stops go beyond the end of the gradient line, then the gradient just stops at whatever point it manages to reach when it gets to the end of the gradient line. This is illustrated in Figure 66:

```
#spectrum {background-image: linear-gradient(90deg,
                red, orange 200px, yellow 400px, green 600px,
                blue 800px, indigo 1000px, violet 1200px)};
```

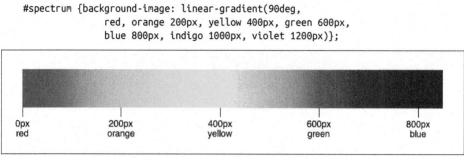

Figure 66. Gradient clipping when colors stops go too far

Since the last color stop is at 1,200 pixels but the gradient line is shorter than that, the gradient just stops right around the color `blue`. That's as far as the gradient gets before running out of room.

Note that in the preceding two examples and figures, the first color (`red`) didn't have a length value. If the first color has no position, it's assumed to be the beginning of the gradient line. Similarly, if you leave a position off the last color stop, it's assumed to be the end of the gradient line.

You can use any length value you like, not just pixels. Ems, inches, you name it. You can even mix different units into the same gradient, although this is not generally recommended for reasons we'll get to in a little bit. You can even have negative length values if you want; doing so will place a color stop before the beginning of the gradient line, and clipping will occur in the same manner as it happens at the end of the line, as shown in Figure 67:

```
#spectrum {background-image: linear-gradient(90deg,
                red -200px, orange 200px, yellow 400px, green 600px,
                blue 800px, indigo 1000px, violet 1200px)};
```

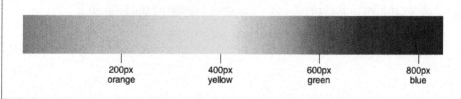

Figure 67. Gradient clipping when color stops have negative positions

As for percentages, they're calculated with respect to the total length of the gradient line. Therefore, a color stop at 50% will be at the midpoint of the gradient line. Let's return to our rainbow example, and instead of having a color stop every 25 pixels, we'll have one every 10% of the gradient line's length. This would look like the following, which has the result shown in Figure 68:

```
#spectrum {background-image: linear-gradient(90deg,
    red, orange 10%, yellow 20%, green 30%, blue 40%, indigo 50%, violet 60%)};
```

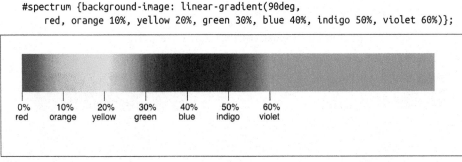

Figure 68. Placing color stops every 10 percent

As we saw previously, since the last color stop comes before the end of the gradient line, its color (`violet`) is carried through to the end of the gradient. These stops are a bit more spread out than the 25-pixel example we saw earlier, but otherwise things happen in more or less the same way.

In cases where some color stops have position values and others don't, the stops without positions are evenly distributed between the ones that do. Consider the following:

```
#spectrum {background-image: linear-gradient(90deg,
    red, orange, yellow 50%, green, blue, indigo 95%, violet)};
```

Because `red` and `violet` don't have specified position values, they're taken to be 0% and 100%, respectively. This means than `orange`, `green`, and `blue` will be evenly distributed between the explicitly defined positions to either side.

For `orange`, that means the point midway between `red 0%` and `yellow 50%`, which is 25%. For `green` and `blue`, these need to be arranged between `yellow 50%` and `indigo 95%`. That's a 45% difference, which is divided in three, because there are three intervals between the four values. That means 65% and 80%. In the end, we get the distorted rainbow shown in Figure 69, exactly as if we'd declared the following:

```
#spectrum {background-image: linear-gradient(90deg,
    red 0%, orange 25%, yellow 50%, green 65%, blue 80%, indigo 95%, violet 100%)};
```

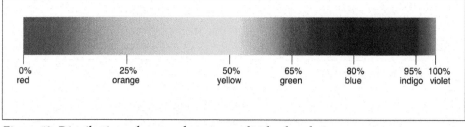

Figure 69. Distributing color stops between explicitly placed stops

This is the same mechanism used to evenly distribute stops along the gradient line when none of them are given a position, of course. If none of the color stops have been positioned, the first is assumed to be 0%, the last is assumed to be 100%, and the other color stops are evenly distributed between those two points.

You might wonder what happens if you mess up and put two color stops at exactly the same point, like this:

```
#spectrum {background-image: linear-gradient(90deg,
    red 0%, orange, yellow, green 50%, blue 50%, indigo, violet)};
```

All that happens is that the two color stops are put on top of each other. The result is shown in Figure 70.

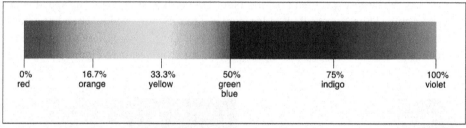

Figure 70. The effect of coincident color stops

The gradient blended as usual all along the gradient line, but at the 50% point, it instantly blended from green to blue over zero length. So the gradient blended from yellow at the 33.3% point (two-thirds of the way from 0% to 50%) to green at the 50% point, then blended from green to blue over zero length, then blended from blue at 50% over to indigo at 75% (midway between 50% and 100%).

This "hard-stop" effect can be useful if you want to create a striped effect, like that shown in Figure 71, which is the result of the following code:

```
.stripes {background-image: linear-gradient(90deg,
    gray 0%, gray 25%,
    transparent 25%, transparent 50%,
    gray 50%, gray 75%,
    transparent 75%, transparent 100%);}
```

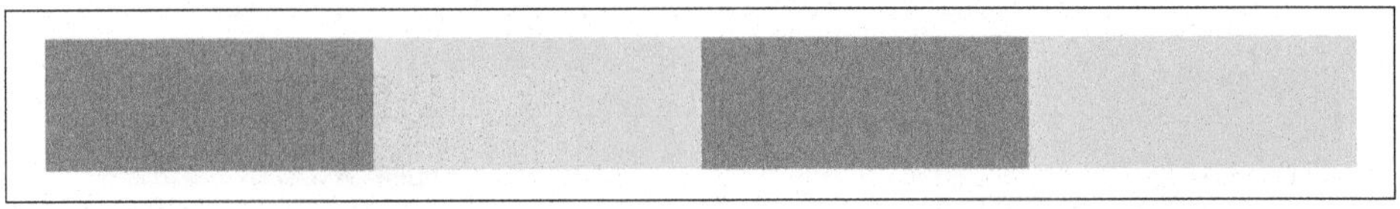

Figure 71. Hard-stop stripes

OK, so that's what happens if you put color stops right on top of each other, but what happens if you put one *before* another? Something like this, say:

```
#spectrum {background-image: linear-gradient(90deg,
    red 0%, orange, yellow, green 50%, blue 40%, indigo, violet)};
```

In that case, the offending color stop (blue in this case) is set to the largest specified value of a preceding color stop. Here, it would be set to 50%, since the stop before it had that position. Thus, the effect is the same as we saw earlier in this section, when the green and blue color stops were placed on top of each other.

The key point here is that the color stop is set to the largest *specified* position of the stop that precedes it. Thus, given the following, the indigo color stop would be set to 50%:

```
#spectrum {background-image: linear-gradient(90deg,
    red 0%, orange, yellow 50%, green, blue, indigo 33%, violet)};
```

In this case, the largest specified position before the indigo stop is the 50% specified at the yellow stop. Thus, the gradient fades from red to orange to yellow, then has a hard switch to indigo before fading from indigo to violet. The gradient's fades from yellow to green to blue to indigo all take place over zero distance. See Figure 72 for the results.

Figure 72. Handling color stops that are out of place

This behavior is the reason why mixing units within a single gradient is generally discouraged. If you mix rems and percentages, for example, you could end up with a situation where a color stop positioned with percentages might end up before an earlier color stop positioned with rems.

As of early 2015, there were bugs in the handling of out-of-place color stops in the Firefox line of browsers.

Gradient lines: the gory details

Now that you have a grasp of the basics of placing color stops, it's time to look closely at how gradient lines are actually constructed, and thus how they create the effects that they do.

First, let's set up a simple gradient so that we can then dissect how it works:

```
linear-gradient(
    55deg, #4097FF, #FFBE00, #4097FF
)
```

Now, how does this one-dimensional construct—a line at 55 degrees on the compass —create a two-dimensional gradient fill? First, the gradient line is placed and its start and ending points determined. This is diagrammed in Figure 73, with the final gradient shown next to it.

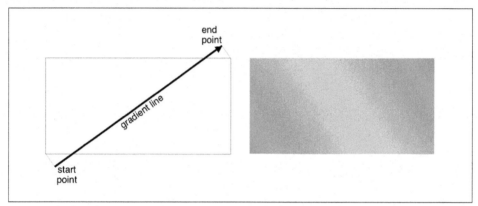

Figure 73. The placement and sizing of the gradient line

The first thing to make very clear is that the box seen here is not an element—it's the linear-gradient image itself. (Remember, we're creating images here.) The size and shape of that image can depend on a lot of things, whether it's the size of the element's background or the application of properties like background-size, which is a topic we'll cover in a bit. For now, we're just concentrating on the image itself.

OK, so in Figure 73, you can see that the gradient line goes straight through the center of the image. The gradient line *always* goes through the center of the gradient image. In this case, we set it to a 55-degree angle, so it's pointing at 55 degrees on the compass. What's interesting are the start and ending points of the gradient line, which are actually outside the image.

Let's talk about the start point first. It's the point on the gradient line where a line perpendicular to the gradient line intersects with the corner of the image furthest away from the gradient line's direction (55deg). Conversely, the gradient line's ending point is the point on the gradient line where a perpendicular line intersects the corner of the image nearest to the gradient line's direction.

Bear in mind that the terms "start point" and "ending point" are a little bit misleading —the gradient line doesn't actually stop at either point. The gradient line is, in fact, infinite. However, the start point is where the first color stop will be placed by default, as it corresponds to position value 0%. Similarly, the ending point corresponds to the position value 100%.

Therefore, given the gradient we defined before:

```
linear-gradient(
    55deg, #4097FF, #FFBE00, #4097FF
)
```

…the color at the start point will be #4097FF, the color at the midpoint (which is also the center of the image) will be #FFBE00, and the color at the ending point will be #4097FF, with smooth blending in between. This is illustrated in Figure 74.

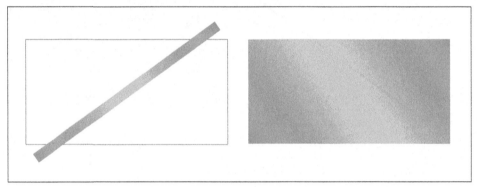

Figure 74. The calculation of color along the gradient line

All right, fine so far. But, you may wonder, how do the bottom-left and top-right corners of the image get set to the same blue that's calculated for the start and ending points, if those points are outside the image? Because the color at each point along the gradient line is extended out perpendicularly from the gradient line. This is partially shown in Figure 75 by extending perpendicular lines at the start and ending points, as well as every 5% of the gradient line between them.

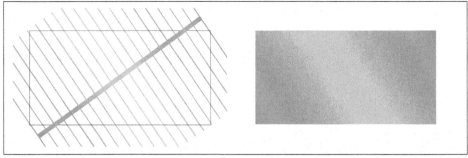

Figure 75. The extension of selected colors along the gradient line

That should be enough to let you fill in the rest mentally, so let's consider what happens to the gradient image in various other settings. We'll use the same gradient definition as before, but this time apply it to wide, square, and tall images. These are shown in Figure 76. Note how the start-point and ending-point colors always make their way into the corners of the gradient image.

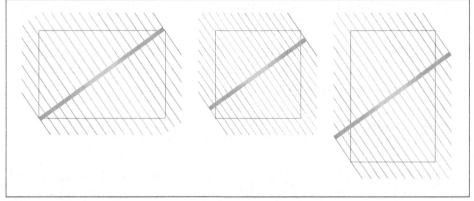

Figure 76. How gradients are constructed for various images

Note how I very carefully said "the start-point and ending-point colors," and did *not* say "the start and end colors." That's because, as we saw earlier, color stops can be placed before the start point and after the ending point, like so:

```
linear-gradient(
    55deg, #4097FF -25%, #FFBE00, #4097FF 125%
)
```

The placement of these color stops as well as the start point and ending point, the way the colors are calculated along the gradient line, and the final gradient are all shown in Figure 77.

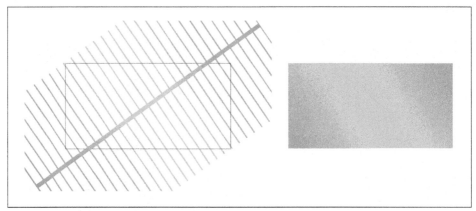

Figure 77. A gradient with stops beyond the start and ending points

Once again, we see that the colors in the bottom-left and top-right corners match the start-point and ending-point colors. It's just that in this case, since the first color stop came before the start point, the actual color at the start point is a blend of the first and second color stops. Likewise for the ending point, which is a blend of the second and third color stops.

Now here's where things get a little bit wacky. Remember how you can use directional keywords, like top and right, to indicate the direction of the gradient line? Suppose you wanted the gradient line to go toward the top right, so you create a gradient image like this:

```
linear-gradient(
    to top right, #4097FF -25%, #FFBE00, #4097FF 125%
)
```

This does *not* cause the gradient line to intersect with the top-right corner. Would that it did! Instead, what happens is a good deal stranger. First, let's diagram it in Figure 78 so that we have something to refer to.

Your eyes do not deceive you: the gradient line is way off from the top-right corner. On the other hand, it *is* headed into the top-right quadrant of the image. That's what to top right really means: head into the top-right quadrant of the image, not into the top-right corner.

As Figure 78 shows, the way to find out exactly what that means is to do the following:

1. Shoot a line from the midpoint of the image into the corners adjacent to the corner in the quadrant that's been declared. Thus, for the top-right quadrant, the adjacent corners are the top left and bottom right.

2. Draw the gradient line perpendicular to that line, pointing into the declared quadrant.

3. Construct the gradient—that is, determine the start and ending points, place or distribute the color stops, then calculate the entire gradient image, as per usual.

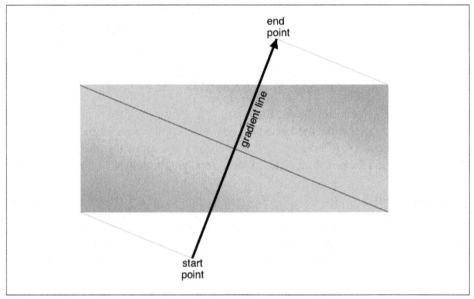

Figure 78. A gradient headed toward the top right

This process has a few interesting side effects. First, it means that the color at the midpoint will always stretch from one quadrant-adjacent corner to the other. Second, it means that if the image's shape changes—that is, if its ratio of height to width changes—then the gradient line will also change direction, meaning that the gradient will reorient. So watch out for that if you have flexible elements. Third, a perfectly square gradient image will have a gradient line that intersects with a corner. Examples of these three side effects are depicted in Figure 79, using the following gradient definition in all three cases:

```
linear-gradient(
    to top right, purple, green 49.5%, black 50%, green 50.5%, gold
)
```

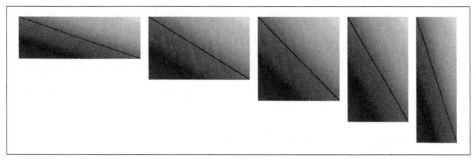

Figure 79. Examples of the side effects of a quadrant-directed gradient

Sadly, there is no way to say "point the gradient line into the corner of a nonsquare image" short of calculating the necessary degree heading yourself and declaring it explicitly, a process that will require JavaScript unless you know the image will always be an exact size in all cases, forever. It's an odd oversight, but one we have to live with.

Radial Gradients

Linear gradients are pretty awesome, but there are times when you really want a circular gradient. You can use such a gradient to create a spotlight effect, a circular shadow, a rounded glow, or any number of other effects. The syntax used is similar to that for linear gradients, but there are some interesting differences:

```
radial-gradient(
    [ [ <shape> || <size> ] [ at <position>]? , | at <position>, ]?
      <color-stop> [, <color-stop> ]+
)
```

What this boils down to is you can optionally declare a shape and size, optionally declare where it center of the gradient is positioned, and then declare two or more color stops. There are some interesting options in the shape and size bits, so let's build up to those.

First, let's look at a simple radial gradient—the simplest possible, in fact—presented in a variety of differently shaped elements (Figure 80):

```
.radial {background-image: radial-gradient(purple, gold);}
```

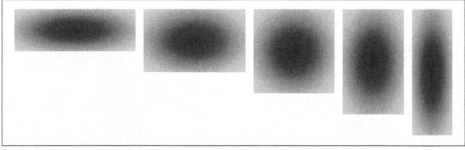

Figure 80. A simple radial gradient in multiple settings

In all of these cases, because no position was declared, the default of center was used. Because no shape was declared, the shape is an ellipse for all cases but the square element; in that case, the shape is a circle. Finally, because no color-stop positions were declared, the first is placed at the beginning of the gradient ray, and the last at the end.

That's right: the *gradient ray*, which is the radial equivalent to the gradient line in linear gradients. It extends outward from the center of the gradient directly to the right, and the rest of the gradient is constructed from it. (We'll get to the details on that in just a bit.)

Shape and size

First off, there are exactly two possible shape values (and thus two possible shapes) for a radial gradient: circle and ellipse. The shape of a gradient can be declared explicitly, or it can be implied by the way you size the gradient image.

So, on to sizing. As always, the simplest way to size a radial gradient is with either one non-negative length (if you're sizing a circle) or two non-negative lengths (if it's an ellipse). Say you have this radial gradient:

```
radial-gradient(50px, purple, gold)
```

This creates a circular radial gradient that fades from purple at the center to gold at a distance of 50 pixels from the center. If we add another length, then the shape becomes an ellipse that's as wide as the first length, and as tall as the second length:

```
radial-gradient(50px 100px, purple, gold)
```

These two gradients are illustrated in Figure 81.

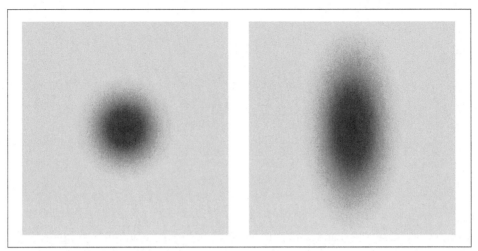

Figure 81. Simple radial gradients

Notice how the shape of the gradients has nothing to do with the overall size and shape of the images in which they appear. If you make a gradient a circle, it will be a circle even if it's inside a rectangular gradient image. So too will an ellipse always be an ellipse, even when inside a square gradient image.

You can also use percentage values for the size, but *only* for ellipses. Circles cannot be given percentage sizes because there's no way to indicate the axis to which that percentage refers. (Imagine an image 100 pixels tall by 500 wide. Should 10% mean 10 pixels or 50 pixels?) If you do supply percentages, then as usual, the first refers to the horizontal axis and the second to the vertical. The following gradient is shown in various settings in Figure 82:

```
radial-gradient(50% 25%, purple, gold)
```

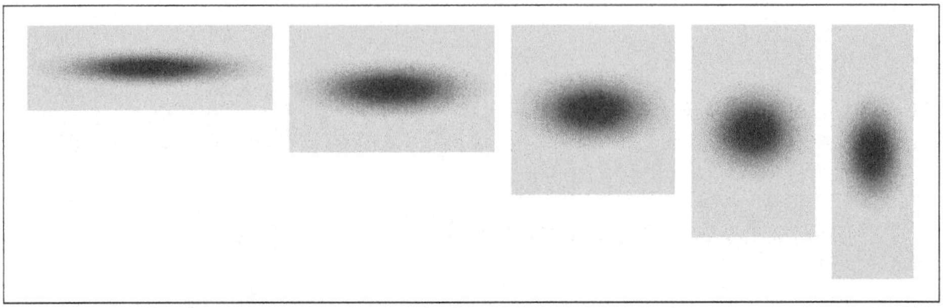

Figure 82. Percentage-sized elliptical gradients

When it comes to ellipses, you're also able to mix lengths and percentages, with the usual caveat to be careful. So if you're feeling confident, you can absolutely make an elliptical radial gradient 10 pixels tall and half the element width, like so:

```
radial-gradient(50% 10px, purple, gold)
```

As it happens, lengths and percentages aren't the only way to size radial gradients. In addition to those value types, there are also four keywords available for sizing radial gradients, the effects of which are summarized in Table 4.

Table 4. Radial gradient sizing keywords

Keyword	Meaning
closest-side	If the radial gradient's shape is a circle, the gradient is sized so that the end of the gradient ray exactly touches the edge of the gradient image that is closest to the center point of the radial gradient. If the shape is an ellipse, then the end of the gradient ray exactly touches the closest edge in each of the horizontal and vertical axes.
farthest-side	If the radial gradient's shape is a circle, the gradient is sized so that the end of the gradient ray exactly touches the edge of the gradient image that is farthest from the center point of the radial gradient. If the shape is an ellipse, then the end of the gradient ray exactly touches the farthest edge in each of the horizontal and vertical axes.
closest-corner	If the radial gradient's shape is a circle, the gradient is sized so that the end of the gradient ray exactly touches the corner of the gradient image that is closest to the center point of the radial gradient. If the shape is an ellipse, then the end of the gradient ray still touches the corner closest to the center, *and* the ellipse has the same aspect ratio that it would have had if closest-side had been specified.
farthest-corner	If the radial gradient's shape is a circle, the gradient is sized so that the end of the gradient ray exactly touches the corner of the gradient image that is farthest from the center point of the radial gradient. If the shape is an ellipse, then the end of the gradient ray still touches the corner farthest from the center, *and* the ellipse has the same aspect ratio that it would have had if farthest-side had been specified. Note: this is the default size value for a radial gradient and so is used if no size values are declared.

In order to better visualize the results of each keyword, see Figure 83, which depicts each keyword applied as both a circle and an ellipse.

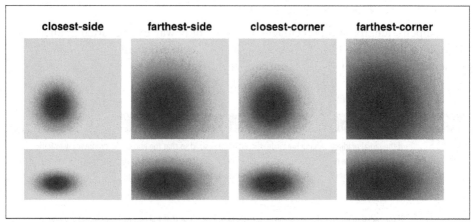

Figure 83. The effects of radial gradient sizing keywords

These keywords cannot be mixed with lengths or percentages in elliptical radial gradients; thus, `closest-side 25px` is invalid and will be ignored.

Something you might have noticed in Figure 83 is that the gradients didn't start at the center of the image. That's because they were positioned elsewhere, which is the topic of the next section.

Positioning radial gradients

If you want to shift the center of a radial gradient away from the default of `center`, then you can do so using any position value that would be valid for `background-position`. I'm not going to reproduce that rather complicated syntax here; flip back to the section on `background-position` ("Background Positioning" on page 17) if you need a refresher.

When I say "any position value that would be valid," that means any permitted combination of lengths, percentages, keywords, and so on. It also means that if you leave off one of the two position values, it will be inferred just the same as for `background-position`. So, just for one example, `center` is equivalent to `center center`.

The one difference between radial gradient positions and background positions is the default: for radial gradients, the default position is `center`, not `0% 0%`. Otherwise, they're the same—and that's really all there is to it.

To give some idea of the possibilities, consider the following rules, illustrated in Figure 84:

```
radial-gradient(at bottom left, purple, gold);
radial-gradient(at center right, purple, gold);
radial-gradient(at 30px 30px, purple, gold);
```

```
radial-gradient(at 25% 66%, purple, gold);
radial-gradient(at 30px 66%, purple, gold);
```

Figure 84. Changing the center position of radial gradients

Of course, none of those positioned radial gradients were explicitly sized, so they all defaulted to farthest-corner. That's a reasonable guess at the intended default behavior, but it's not the only possibility. Let's mix some sizes into the gradients we just saw and find out how that changes things (as depicted in Figure 85):

```
radial-gradient(30px at bottom left, purple, gold);
radial-gradient(30px 15px at center right, purple, gold);
radial-gradient(50% 15% at 30px 30px, purple, gold);
radial-gradient(farthest-side at 25% 66%, purple, gold);
radial-gradient(farthest-corner at 30px 66%, purple, gold);
```

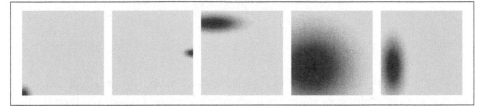

Figure 85. Changing the center position of explicitly sized radial gradients

Nifty. Now, suppose we want something a little more complicated than a fade from one color to another. Next stop, color stops!

Radial color stops and the gradient ray

Color stops for radial gradients work in a similar fashion to linear gradients. Let's return to the simplest possible radial gradient and follow it with a more explicit equivalent:

```
radial-gradient(purple, gold);
radial-gradient(purple 0%, gold 100%);
```

So the gradient ray extends out from the center point. At 0% (the start point, and also the center of the gradient), the ray will be purple. At 100% (the ending point), the ray will be gold. Between the two stops is a smooth blend from purple to gold; beyond the ending point, solid gold.

If we add a stop between purple and gold, but don't give it a position, then it will be placed midway between them, and the blending will be altered accordingly, as shown in Figure 86:

```
radial-gradient(purple 0%, green, gold 100%);
```

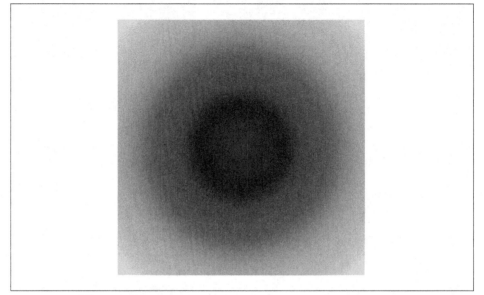

Figure 86. Adding a color stop

We'd have gotten the same result if we'd added green 50% there, but you get the idea. The gradient ray's color goes smoothly from purple to green to gold, and then is solid gold beyond that point on the ray.

This illustrates one difference between gradient lines (for linear gradients) and gradient rays: a linear gradient is derived by extending the color at each point along the gradient line off perpendicular to the gradient line. A similar behavior occurs with a radial gradient, except in that case, they aren't lines that come off the gradient ray. Instead, they are ellipses that are scaled-up or scaled-down versions of the ellipse at the ending point. This is illustrated in Figure 87, where an ellipse shows its gradient ray and then the ellipses that are drawn at various points along that ray.

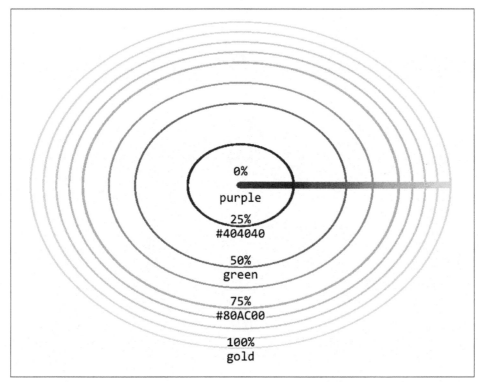

Figure 87. The gradient ray and some of the ellipses it spawns

That brings up an interesting question: how is the ending point (the 100% point, if you like) determined for each gradient ray? Simply, it's the point where the gradient ray intersects with the shape described by the size. In the case of a circle, that's easy: the gradient ray's ending point is however far from the center that the size value indicates. So for a 25px circle gradient, the ending point of the ray is 25 pixels from the center.

For an ellipse, it's essentially the same operation, except that the distance from the center is dependent on the horizontal axis of the ellipse. Given a radial gradient that's a 40px 20px ellipse, the ending point will be 40 pixels from the center and directly to its right. Figure 88 shows this in some detail.

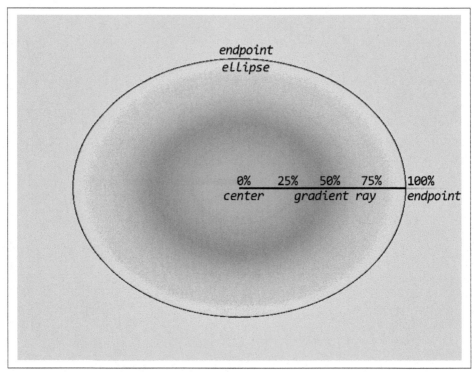

Figure 88. Setting the gradient ray's ending point

Another difference between linear gradient lines and radial gradient rays is that you can see beyond the ending point. If you recall, a linear gradient line is always drawn so that you can see the colors at the 0% and 100% points, but nothing beyond them; the gradient line can never be any smaller than the longest axis of the gradient image, and will frequently be longer than that. With a radial gradient, on the other hand, you can size the radial shape to be smaller than the total gradient image. In that case, the color at the last color stop is simply extended outward from the ending point. (We've already seen this in several previous figures.)

Conversely, if you set a color stop that's beyond the ending point of a ray, you might get to see the color out to that stop. Consider the following gradient, illustrated in Figure 89:

```
radial-gradient(50px circle at center, purple, green, gold 80px)
```

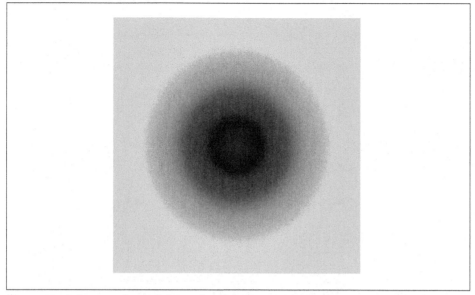

Figure 89. Color stops beyond the ending point

The first color stop has no position, so it's set to 0%, which is the center point. The last color stop is set to 80px, so it will be 80 pixels away from the center in all directions. The middle color stop, green, is placed midway between the two (40 pixels from the center). So we get a gradient that goes out to gold at 80 pixels and then continues gold beyond that point.

This happens even though the circle was explicitly set to be 50 pixels large. It still is 50 pixels in radius, it's just that the positioning of the last color stop makes that fact vaguely irrelevant. Visually, we might as well have declared this:

```
radial-gradient(80px circle at center, purple, green, gold)
```

or, more simply, just this:

```
radial-gradient(80px, purple, green, gold)
```

The same behaviors apply if you use percentages for your color stops. These are equivalent to the previous examples, and to each other, visually speaking:

```
radial-gradient(50px, purple, green, gold 160%)
radial-gradient(80px, purple, green, gold 100%)
```

Now, what if you set a negative position for a color stop? It's pretty much the same result as we saw with linear gradient lines: the negative color stop is used to figure out the color at the start point, but is otherwise unseen. Thus, the following gradient will have the result shown in Figure 90:

```
radial-gradient(80px, purple -40px, green, gold)
```

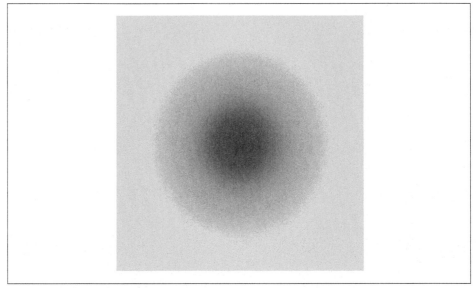

Figure 90. Handling a negative color-stop position

Given these color-stop positions, the first color stop is at -40px, the last is at 80px (because, given its lack of an explicit position, it defaults to the ending point), and the middle is placed midway between them. The result is the same as if we'd explicitly said:

```
radial-gradient(80px, purple -40px, green 20px, gold 80px)
```

That's why the color at the center of the gradient is a green-purple: it's a blend of one-third purple, two-thirds green. From there, it blends the rest of the way to green, and then on to gold. The rest of the purple-green blend, the part that sits on the "negative space" of the gradient ray, is invisible.

Degenerate cases

Given that we can declare size and position for a radial gradient, the question arises: what if a circular gradient has zero radius, or an elliptical gradient has zero height or width? These conditions aren't quite as hard to create as you might think: besides simply explicitly declaring that a radial gradient has zero size using 0px or 0%, you could also do something like this:

```
radial-gradient(closest-corner circle at top right, purple, gold)
```

The gradient's size is set to closest-corner, and the center has been moved into the top right corner, so the closest corner is zero pixels away from the center. Now what?

In this case, the specification very explicitly says that the gradient should be rendered as if it's "a circle whose radius [is] an arbitrary very small number greater than zero." So that might mean as if it had a radius of one-one-billionth of a pixel, or a picometer, or heck, the Planck length. (Kids, ask your science teacher.) The interesting thing is that it means the gradient is still a circle. It's just a very, very, very small circle. Probably, it will be too small to actually render anything visible. If so, you'll just get a solid-color fill that corresponds to the color of the last color stop instead.

Ellipses with zero-length dimensions have fascinatingly different defined behaviors. Let's assume the following:

```
radial-gradient(0px 50% at center, purple, gold)
```

The specification states that any ellipse with a zero width is rendered as if it's "an ellipse whose height [is] an arbitrary very large number and whose width [is] an arbitrary very small number greater than zero." In other words, render it as though it's a linear gradient mirrored around the vertical axis running through the center of the ellipse. The specification also says that in such a case, any color stops with percentage positions resolve to 0px. This will usually result in a solid color matching the color defined for the last color stop.

On the other hand, if you use lengths to position the color stops, you can get a vertically mirrored horizontal linear gradient for free. Consider the following gradient, illustrated in Figure 91:

```
radial-gradient(0px 50% at center, purple 0px, gold 100px)
```

Figure 91. The effects of a zero-width ellipse

How did this happen? First, remember that the specification says that the 0px horizontal width is treated as it it's a tiny non-zero number. For the sake of illustration, let's suppose that's one-one-thousandth of a pixel (0.001px). That means the ellipse shape is a thousandth of a pixel wide by half the height of the image. Again for the sake of illustration, let's suppose that's a height of 100 pixels. That means the first ellipse shape is a thousandth of a pixel wide by 100 pixels tall, which is an aspect ratio of 0.001:100, or 1:100,000.

Okay, so every ellipse drawn along the gradient ray has a 1:100,000 aspect ratio. That means the ellipse at half a pixel along the gradient ray is one pixel wide and 100,000 pixels tall. At one pixel, it's two pixels wide and 200,000 pixels tall. At five pixels, the ellipse is 10 pixels by a million pixels. At fifty pixels along the gradient ray, the ellipse is 100 pixels wide and ten million tall. And so on. This is diagrammed in Figure 92.

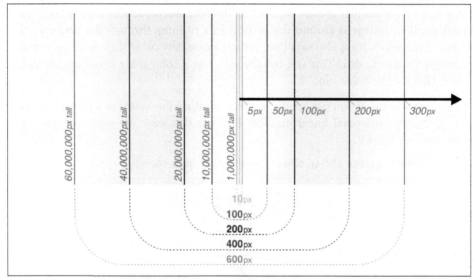

Figure 92. Very, very tall ellipses

So you can see why the visual effect is of a mirrored linear gradient. These ellipses are effectively drawing vertical lines. Technically they aren't, but in practical terms they are. Therefore, the result is as if you have a vertically mirrored horizontal gradient, because each ellipse is centered on the center of the gradient, and both sides of it get drawn. While this may be a radial gradient, we can't see its radial nature.

On the other hand, if the ellipse has width but not height, the results are quite different. You'd think the result would be to have a vertical linear gradient mirrored around the horizontal axis, but not so! Instead, the result is a solid color equal to the last color stop. (Unless it's a repeating gradient, a subject we'll turn to shortly, in which case it should be a solid color equal to the average color of the gradient.) So, given either of the following, you'll get a solid gold:

```
radial-gradient(50% 0px at center, purple, gold)
radial-gradient(50% 0px at center, purple 0px, gold 100px)
```

Why the difference? It goes back to how radial gradients are constructed from the gradient ray. Again, remember that, per the specification, a zero distance here is treated as a very small non-zero number. As before, we'll assume that `0px` is reassigned to `0.001px`, and that the `50%` evaluates to 100 pixels. That's an aspect ratio of 100:0.001, or 100,000:1.

So, to get an ellipse that's one pixel tall, the width of that ellipse must be 100,000 pixels. But our last color stop is only at 100 pixels! At that point, the ellipse that's drawn is 100 pixels wide and a thousandth of a pixel tall. All of the purple-to-gold transition that happens along the gradient ray has to happen in that thousandth of a pixel. Everything after that is gold, as per the final color stop. Thus, we can only see the gold.

You might think that if you increased the position value of the last color stop to `100000px`, you'd see a thin sliver of purple-ish color running horizontally across the image. And you'd be right, *if* the browser treats `0px` as `0.001px` in these cases. If it assumes `0.00000001px` instead, you'd have to increase the color stop's position a *lot* further in order to see anything. And that's assuming the browser was actually caulculating and drawing all those ellipses, instead of just hard-coding the special cases. The latter is a lot more likely, honestly. It's what I'd do if I were in charge of a browser's gradient-rendering code.

And what if an ellipse has zero width *and* zero height? In that case, the specification is written such that the zero-width behavior is used; thus, you'll get the mirrored-linear-gradient behavior.

 As of early 2015, browser support for the defined behavior in these edge cases was unstable, at best. Some browsers used the last color-stop's color in all cases, and others simply refused to draw a gradient at all in some cases.

Manipulating Gradient Images

As has been emphasized (possibly to excess), gradients are images. That means you can size, position, repeat, and otherwise affect them with the various background properties, just as you would any PNG or SVG.

One way this can be leveraged is to repeat simple gradients. (Repeating in more complex ways is the subject of the next section.) For example, you could use a hard-stop radial gradient to give your background a dotted look, as shown in Figure 92:

```
body {background: tan center/25px 25px repeat
    radial-gradient(circle at center,
                rgba(0,0,0,0.1), rgba(0,0,0,0.1) 10px,
                transparent 10px, transparent);}
```

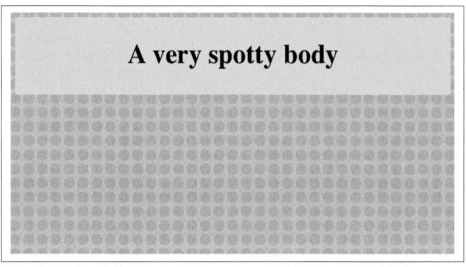

Figure 93. Tiled radial gradient images

Yes, this is visually pretty much the same as tiling a PNG that has a mostly-transparent dark circle 10 pixels in diameter. There are three advantages to using a gradient in this case:

- The CSS is almost certainly smaller in bytes than the PNG would be.
- Even more importantly, the PNG requires an extra hit on the server. This slows down both page and server performance. A CSS gradient is part of the stylesheet and so eliminates the extra server hit.
- Changing the gradient is a lot simpler, so experimenting to find exactly the right size, shape, and darkness is much easier.

Of course, gradients can't do everything a raster or vector image can, so it's not as though you'll be giving up external images completely now that gradients are a thing. You can still pull off some pretty impressive effects with gradients, though. Consider the background effect shown in Figure 94.

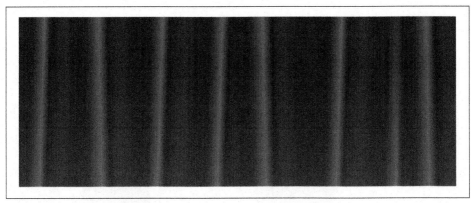

Figure 94. It's time to start the music...

That curtain effect was accomplished with just two linear gradients repeated at differing intervals, plus a third to create a "glow" effect along the bottom of the background. Here's the code that accomplished it:

```
background-image:
    linear-gradient(0deg, rgba(255,128,128,0.25), transparent 75%),
    linear-gradient(89deg,
        transparent, transparent 30%,
        #510A0E 35%, #510A0E 40%, #61100F 43%, #B93F3A 50%,
        #4B0408 55%, #6A0F18 60%, #651015 65%, #510A0E 70%,
        #510A0E 75%, rgba(255,128,128,0) 80%, transparent),
    linear-gradient(92deg,
        #510A0E, #510A0E 20%, #61100F 25%, #B93F3A 40%, #4B0408 50%,
        #6A0F18 70%, #651015 80%, #510A0E 90%, #510A0E);
background-size: auto, 300px 100%, 109px 100%;
background-repeat: repeat-x;
```

The first (and therefore topmost) gradient is just a fade from a 75%-transparent light red up to full transparency at the 75% point of the gradient line. Then two "fold" images are created. Figure 95 shows each separately.

With those images defined, they are repeated along the X (horizontal) axis and given different sizes. The first, which is the "glow" effect, is given auto size in order to let it cover the entire element background. The second is given a width of 300px and a height of 100%; thus, it will be as tall as the element background and 300 pixels wide. This means it will be tiled every 300 pixels along the X axis. The same is true of the third image, except it tiles every 109 pixels. The end result looks like an irregular stage curtain.

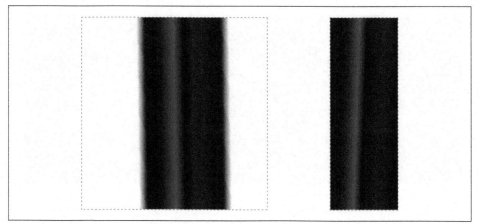

Figure 95. The two "fold" gradients

The beauty of this is that adjusting the tiling intervals is just a matter of editing the stylesheet. Changing the color-stop positions or the colors is less trivial, but not too difficult if you know what effect you're after. And, of course, adding a third set of repeating folds is no more difficult than just adding another gradient to the stack.

Repeating Gradients

Gradients are pretty awesome by themselves, but because they are images, they can be subject to strange behaviors when they are tiled. For example, if you declare:

```
h1.exmpl {background:
    linear-gradient(-45deg, black 0, black 25px, yellow 25px, yellow 50px)
    top left/40px 40px repeat;}
```

...then you could easily end up with a situation like that shown in Figure 96.

Figure 96. Tiling gradient images with background-repeat

As the figure shows, there is a discontinuity where the images repeat. You *could* try to nail down the exact sizes of the element and gradient image and then mess with the construction of the gradient image in order to try to make the sides line up, but it would be a lot better if there was just a way to say, "repeat this seamlessly forever."

Enter repeating gradients. For the previous example, all we need is to convert linear-gradient to repeating-linear-gradient and drop the background-size value. Everything else about the code stays the same. The effect is much different, however, as you can see in Figure 97:

```
h1.exmpl {background: repeating-linear-gradient(-45deg,
        black 0, black 25px, yellow 25px, yellow 50px) top left;}
```

Figure 97. A repeating gradient image with repeating-linear-gradient

What happens with a repeating linear gradient is that the declared color stops are repeated on a loop along the gradient line, over and over, forever. Given the previous example, that means switching between black and yellow every 25 pixels forever.

Now, that example worked because there was supposed to be a hard stop where the gradient repeated. If you're using smoother transitions, you need to be careful that the color value at the last color stop matches the color value at the first color stop. Consider this:

```
repeating-linear-gradient(-45deg, purple 0px, gold 50px)
```

This will produce a smooth gradient from purple to gold at 50 pixels, and then a hard switch back to purple and another 50-pixel purple-to-gold blend. By adding one more color stop with the same color as the first color stop, the gradient can be smoothed out to avoid hard-stop lines. See Figure 98 for a comparison of the two approaches:

```
repeating-linear-gradient(-45deg, purple 0px, gold 50px, purple 100px)
```

Figure 98. Dealing with hard resets in repeating-gradient images

You may have noticed that none of the repeating gradients we've seen so far have a defined size. That means the images are defaulting in size to the full background positioning area of the element to which they're applied, per the default behavior for images that have no intrinsic height and width. Of course, if you were to resize a repeating-gradient image using background-size, the repeating gradient would only be visible within the gradient image. If you then repeated it using background-repeat, you could very easily be back to the situation of having discontinuities in your background, as illustrated in Figure 99:

```
h1.exmpl {background:
    repeating-linear-gradient(-45deg, purple 0px, gold 50px, purple 100px)
    top left/50px 50px repeat;}
```

Figure 99. Repeated tiling of repeating-gradient images

If you use percentages in your repeating linear gradients, they'll be placed the same as if the gradient wasn't of the repeating variety. Then again, this would mean that all of the gradients defined by those color stops would be seen and none of the repetitions would be visible, so percentages are kind of pointless with repeating linear gradients.

On the other hand, percentages can be very useful with repeating radial gradients, where the size of the circle or ellipse is defined, percentage positions along the gradient ray are defined, and you can see beyond the endpoint of the gradient ray. For example, assume:

```
.ex02 {background:
    repeating-radial-gradient(100px 50px, purple, gold 20%, green 40%,
                              purple 60%, yellow 80%, purple);}
```

Given this rule, there will be a color stop every 20 pixels, with the colors repeating in the declared pattern. Because the first and last color stops have the same color value, there is no hard color switch. The ripples just spread out forever, or at least until they're beyond the edges of the gradient image. See Figure 100 for an example.

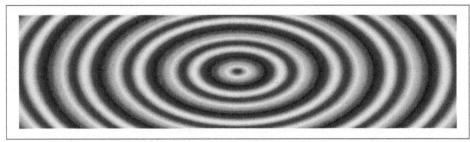

Figure 100. Repeating radial gradients

Just imagine what that would look like with a repeating radial gradient of a rainbow!

```
.wdim {background:
    repeating-radial-gradient(
        100px circle at bottom center,
        rgb(83%,83%,83%) 50%,
        violet 55%, indigo 60%, blue 65%, green 70%,
        yellow 75%, orange 80%, red 85%,
        rgb(47%,60%,73%) 90%
    );}
```

There are a couple of things to keep in mind when creating repeating radial gradients:

- If you don't declare size dimensions for a radial, it will default to an ellipse that has the same height-to-width ratio as the overall gradient image; *and*, if you don't declare a size for the image with `background-size`, the gradient image will default to the height and width of the element background where it's being applied. (Or, in the case of being used as a list-style bullet, the size that the browser gives it.)

- The default radial size value is `farthest-corner`. This will put the endpoint of the gradient ray far enough to the right that its ellipse intersects with the corner of the gradient image that's furthest from the center point of the radial gradient.

These are reiterated here to remind you that if you stick to the defaults, there's not really any point to having a repeating gradient, since you'll only be able to see the first iteration of the repeat. It's only when you restrict the initial size of the gradient that the repeats become visible.

 Radial gradients, and in particular repeating radial gradients, can be a massive performance drain for mobile devices. Crashes have not been uncommon in these situations, and both page rendering time and battery performance can suffer greatly. Think very, very carefully about using radial gradients in mobile contexts, and be sure to rigorously test their performance and stability in any context.

Average gradient colors

Another edge case is what happens if a repeating gradient's first and last color stops somehow end up being in the same place. For example, suppose your fingers missed the "5" key and you accidentally declared the following:

```
repeating-radial-gradient(center, purple 0px, gold 0px)
```

The first and last color stops are zero pixels apart, but the gradient is supposed to repeat ad infinitum along the gradient line. Now what?

In such a case, the browser finds the *average gradient color* and fills it in throughout the entire gradient image. In our simple case in the preceding code, that will be a 50/50 blend of purple and gold (which will be about #C06C40 or rgb(75%,42%,25%)). Thus, the resulting gradient image should be a solid orangey-brown, which doesn't really look much like a gradient.

This condition can also be triggered in cases where the browser rounds the color-stop positions to zero, or cases where the distance between the first and last color stops is so small as compared to the output resolution that nothing useful can be rendered. This could happen if, for example, a repeating radial gradient used all percentages for the color-stop positions and was sized using `closest-side`, but was accidentally placed into a corner.

 As of early 2015, no browsers really do this correctly. It is possible to trigger some of the correct behaviors in Firefox under very limited conditions, but in most cases, browsers either just use the last color stop as a fill color, or else try really hard to draw sub-pixel repeating patterns. This often causes browser crashes, so be very careful to avoid situations that might trigger average-color behavior!

Summary

Setting colors and backgrounds on elements gives authors a great deal of power. The advantage of CSS over traditional methods is that colors and backgrounds can be applied to any element in a document.

About the Author

Eric A. Meyer has been working with the Web since late 1993 and is an internationally recognized expert on the subjects of HTML, CSS, and web standards. A widely read author, he is also the founder of Complex Spiral Consulting (*http://www.complex spiral.com*), which counts among its clients America Online; Apple Computer, Inc.; Wells Fargo Bank; and Macromedia, which described Eric as "a critical partner in our efforts to transform Macromedia Dreamweaver MX 2004 into a revolutionary tool for CSS-based design."

Beginning in early 1994, Eric was the visual designer and campus web coordinator for the Case Western Reserve University website, where he also authored a widely acclaimed series of three HTML tutorials and was project coordinator for the online version of the *Encyclopedia of Cleveland History* and the *Dictionary of Cleveland Biography*, the first encyclopedia of urban history published fully and freely on the Web.

Author of *Eric Meyer on CSS* and *More Eric Meyer on CSS* (New Riders), *CSS: The Definitive Guide* (*http://bit.ly/css-tdg-3e*) (O'Reilly), and *CSS2.0 Programmer's Reference* (Osborne/McGraw-Hill), as well as numerous articles for the O'Reilly Network, Web Techniques, and Web Review, Eric also created the CSS Browser Compatibility Charts and coordinated the authoring and creation of the W3C's official CSS Test Suite. He has lectured to a wide variety of organizations, including Los Alamos National Laboratory, the New York Public Library, Cornell University, and the University of Northern Iowa. Eric has also delivered addresses and technical presentations at numerous conferences, among them An Event Apart (which he cofounded), the IW3C2 WWW series, Web Design World, CMP, SXSW, the User Interface conference series, and The Other Dreamweaver Conference.

In his personal time, Eric acts as list chaperone of the highly active css-discuss mailing list (*http://www.css-discuss.org*), which he cofounded with John Allsopp of Western Civilisation, and which is now supported by *evolt.org*. Eric lives in Cleveland, Ohio, which is a much nicer city than you've been led to believe. For nine years he was the host of "Your Father's Oldsmobile," a big-band radio show heard weekly on WRUW 91.1 FM in Cleveland.

You can find more detailed information on Eric's personal web page (*http://www.meyerweb.com/eric*).

Colophon

The animals on the cover of *Colors, Backgrounds, and Gradients* are salmon (*salmonidae*), which is a family of fish consisting of many different species. Two of the most common salmon are the Pacific salmon and the Atlantic salmon.

Pacific salmon live in the northern Pacific Ocean off the coasts of North America and Asia. There are five subspecies of Pacific salmon, with an average weight of 10 to 30 pounds. Pacific salmon are born in the fall in freshwater stream gravel beds, where they incubate through the winter and emerge as inch-long fish. They live for a year or two in streams or lakes and then head downstream to the ocean. There they live for a few years, before heading back upstream to their exact place of birth to spawn and then die.

Atlantic salmon live in the northern Atlantic Ocean off the coasts of North America and Europe. There are many subspecies of Atlantic salmon, including the trout and the char. Their average weight is 10 to 20 pounds. The Atlantic salmon family has a life cycle similar to that of its Pacific cousins, and also travels from freshwater gravel beds to the sea. A major difference between the two, however, is that the Atlantic salmon does not die after spawning; it can return to the ocean and then return to the stream to spawn again, usually two or three times.

Salmon, in general, are graceful, silver-colored fish with spots on their backs and fins. Their diet consists of plankton, insect larvae, shrimp, and smaller fish. Their unusually keen sense of smell is thought to help them navigate from the ocean back to the exact spot of their birth, upstream past many obstacles. Some species of salmon remain landlocked, living their entire lives in freshwater.

Salmon are an important part of the ecosystem, as their decaying bodies provide fertilizer for streambeds. Their numbers have been dwindling over the years, however. Factors in the declining salmon population include habitat destruction, fishing, dams that block spawning paths, acid rain, droughts, floods, and pollution.

The cover image is a 19th-century engraving from the Dover Pictorial Archive. The cover fonts are URW Typewriter and Guardian Sans. The text font is Adobe Minion Pro; the heading font is Adobe Myriad Condensed; and the code font is Dalton Maag's Ubuntu Mono.

Get even more for your money.

Join the O'Reilly Community, and register the O'Reilly books you own. It's free, and you'll get:

- $4.99 ebook upgrade offer
- 40% upgrade offer on O'Reilly print books
- Membership discounts on books and events
- Free lifetime updates to ebooks and videos
- Multiple ebook formats, DRM FREE
- Participation in the O'Reilly community
- Newsletters
- Account management
- 100% Satisfaction Guarantee

Signing up is easy:

1. Go to: oreilly.com/go/register
2. Create an O'Reilly login.
3. Provide your address.
4. Register your books.

Note: English-language books only

To order books online:
oreilly.com/store

For questions about products or an order:
orders@oreilly.com

To sign up to get topic-specific email announcements and/or news about upcoming books, conferences, special offers, and new technologies:
elists@oreilly.com

For technical questions about book content:
booktech@oreilly.com

To submit new book proposals to our editors:
proposals@oreilly.com

O'Reilly books are available in multiple DRM-free ebook formats. For more information:
oreilly.com/ebooks

CPSIA information can be obtained at www.ICGtesting.com
Printed in the USA
LVOW02s1458300615

444443LV00003B/8/P

9 781491 927656